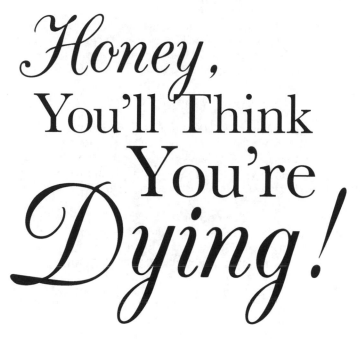

Honey, You'll Think You're Dying!

It's Not Death, It's Just Panic

LISA TUCKER

WESTBOW
PRESS®
A DIVISION OF THOMAS NELSON
& ZONDERVAN

Scripture taken from the King James Version of the Bible.

Scripture quotations marked (NIV) are taken from the Holy Bible, New International Version®, NIV®. Copyright © 1973, 1978, 1984, 2011 by Biblica, Inc.™ Used by permission of Zondervan. All rights reserved worldwide. www.zondervan.com The "NIV" and "New International Version" are trademarks registered in the United States Patent and Trademark Office by Biblica, Inc.™

This book is a work of non-fiction. Unless otherwise noted, the author and the publisher make no explicit guarantees as to the accuracy of the information contained in this book and in some cases, names of people and places have been altered to protect their privacy.

WestBow Press books may be ordered through booksellers or by contacting:

WestBow Press
A Division of Thomas Nelson & Zondervan
1663 Liberty Drive
Bloomington, IN 47403
www.westbowpress.com
1 (866) 928-1240

Because of the dynamic nature of the Internet, any web addresses or links contained in this book may have changed since publication and may no longer be valid. The views expressed in this work are solely those of the author and do not necessarily reflect the views of the publisher, and the publisher hereby disclaims any responsibility for them.

Any people depicted in stock imagery provided by Thinkstock are models, and such images are being used for illustrative purposes only. Certain stock imagery © Thinkstock.

ISBN: 978-1-9736-1778-5 (sc)
ISBN: 978-1-9736-1780-8 (hc)
ISBN: 978-1-9736-1779-2 (e)

Library of Congress Control Number: 2018901382

Print information available on the last page.

WestBow Press rev. date: 02/21/2018

DEDICATION

To my husband, my soul mate, Brad, who in sickness and in health stood firmly by my side. You were so giving and supportive with every sacrifice. I love and adore you. Thank you

Lisa and Brad

To my beautiful daughter, Alicia, who missed many outings and trips to the mall with Mom. I cherish every moment we spend together. I love you!

To my son-in-law, Kevin. may Christ continue to grow and bless you.

Alicia and Kevin

To my precious gifts, my grandchildren, Taylor, Mallorie, Brett and Camrynn. God has blessed me enormously! "Dee" loves you so....

ACKNOWLEDGMENTS

A special thanks to my family and friends who have supported me, took time out to have lunch with me, drove me to pick up Alicia from school, drove me to the store, ran errands without question, and prayed continuously. Thanks to my family and friends who called to prevent me from being lonely.

To my girlfriends: Denise, Sonya, Darlene, Karen, Jeanette, Susan, Judy, Angie, Robin, and Laura. I'm grateful for our friendships. I am blessed.

A special thank you to Beth Moore who followed God's will in writing the Bible study "Esther, It's Tough Being a Woman." Through that study I became inspired to become transparent and give my heart and life experiences in this book.

CONTENTS

FOREWORD

Queen Esther, one of the famous women of the Bible, is a woman who knows what it feels like to look straight into the face of fear. She was the only one who could save the Jews from total annihilation after her husband, King Xerxes, signed an edict to have them destroyed. She knew her very own life was at stake, and she was scared to death. But during the crisis, she also realized that she had "come to royal position for such a time as this" (Esther 4:14). She did not let her fears control her actions, and, ultimately, the Jews were saved. Esther had accomplished what God put her on this earth to do.

But it's not always easy to win the battle over fear. Fear can control you if you allow it. If anyone knows that to be a fact, it's my mom. She has battled with fear most of her life in the form of anxiety, panic attacks, and agoraphobia. In order to try to live a normal life, she too has been forced to face fear. On some days, it took everything she had just to leave her own home. And even though people ridiculed her and she was tempted to self-diagnose herself as a lunatic, God had His loving hand on her through it all.

Psalm 16:5 says "Lord, you have assigned me my portion and my cup; you have made my lot secure." In other words, the cards you've been dealt are from God. He knows everything you're going through, and it is all for His purpose. "No matter what life—or Satan himself—hands us, the favor God has on His children causes that 'lot' to tumble out on the table in such a way that, instead of destruction, the child will discover that [his] portion turned into destiny one trusting step at a time. When all is said and done, [you] will see that the portion God assigned was good. Right. Rich. Full of purpose" (Beth Moore).

"Esther, It's Tough Being a Woman" is a wonderful Bible study written by Beth Moore.

Through the study, the Lord showed my mom what she believes is the purpose of the "portion" He assigned to her: this very book you hold in your hands. This book gives a glimpse inside the secret areas of Mom's life that, for so many years, she's tried to hide. Although she has not conquered all of her fears, her phobias have not destroyed her. She's still breathing, which means God isn't finished with her yet. If her story helps you conquer your own battle with fear, her "portion" has not been in vain. Her life is rich and full of purpose- and she wants to share it with you on these pages.

The author's daughter, Alicia Wiggins

Alicia

(To serve God is to serve others. And to serve others is to serve purpose.)
Beth Moore

INTRODUCTION

*A*s I sat here this evening looking back on when this adventure began, I realized that when you think you're ready to take on a task, God is not always on your time frame. I began writing this book in 1994 with great hope that I could help someone else along the way by sharing my personal experiences. Since that time, God has grown me in many areas of my life, so here I begin again.

As a child of God, knowing he loves me and that I have a home in heaven doesn't make me or any other believer exempt from hardships. This book is about an agoraphobic woman who has lived a great amount of time held captive to fear. That woman is me.

My name is Lisa Tucker. I was born and raised in the state of Georgia. I am the eighth child of eleven children. I grew up in a big family, going to school and church, and playing with my friends. I was raised by my parents and my grandmother, Bert, who lived with our family until the day she died. My Father, Vernon, is a Baptist minister and a former marine sergeant. As my eldest brother, Mike, described so well: Dad represented the "law" in our home. My Mom, Johnnie, spent her time supporting my dad in his ministry and working to help provide for our very large family. Mike refers to her role in our growing up years as "grace."

I am a fifty six-year-old woman who has struggled with panic attacks and agoraphobia for years. In 1994 I thought I was given the answer that would free me from this terror. I pray that through your readings you may gain information that could help a friend, family member, or maybe even yourself. Knowledge truly is power and a huge step in overcoming any obstacle we may face.

As I have grown up in the home of a Baptist minister, I've come to the conclusion with this often asked question, "Does God *always* remove bad things in our lives?" I can tell you no, not always. Sometimes He chooses to grow and shape us instead. He uses our lives and circumstances, if we allow Him, to reach out to those who will come behind giving them a hope that they too can make it. Your struggles are for someone else.

My journey still continues—this I share with you...

Lisa's parents and all eleven children. Left to right: Mike, Roger, Linda, Dondra, Karen, David, Steve, me(Lisa), Leslie, Greg, Jason. Parents: Mom(Johnnie), Dad(Vernon)

OUR DREAMS COMING TRUE

I met my husband, Brad, just prior to turning the age of fourteen. His father, Alvin, attended the church where my father was ministering at the time. Alvin asked Brad on numerous occasions to visit our church. Brad finally accepted the invite, and after meeting the youth of the church he began coming on a regular basis. (I have to add here that he said when he first saw me he knew he'd be back.) We were introduced at one of the youth outings, and that is where our relationship began. As we got to know each other better, we also discovered that we attended the same high school and knew one another's siblings but had no knowledge each other existed.

We started dating and eventually fell in love, becoming "high school sweethearts." After dating for a year, Brad proposed. I accepted, and we planned all through high school to be married. Our dream was to get married after we graduated and raise a family. We fantasized about having the perfect home filled with love and at least three children. I never planned on furthering my education by going on to college; I never considered it. Things were different when I was young. I don't think women were as career-oriented as they are today. "What kind of wife and mother are you going to be if you can't cook, clean, and take care of children?" Those were the words my father would ask, and like many girls of that era, this attitude greatly shaped my ideas for the future.

Brad and Lisa dating

Brad graduated in 1976 and began working fulltime. I was still in school and worked part-time jobs. Sometimes I helped my mom by relieving her in the afternoons at a company called North Center. I'll never forget my first job at Burger King. My mom decided to bring my three younger siblings to see me at work. They ordered milkshakes, and as I began filling their cups, the milkshake machine wouldn't shut off. Milkshake was pouring from the cups and overflowing onto the floor. I kept shoving cup after cup trying to capture the mess. Everybody was laughing, including my mom!

Lisa in Burger King uniform

During my senior year of high school, I began searching for the perfect wedding gown. When I found the dress, I returned many times to try it on again and again. I made payments on it with money from my part-time job and graduation money I had received as gifts; I'll never forget the elation of walking into the Crystal Bridal Shop at the Belvedere Plaza to make the final purchase for my wedding dress. On June 6, 1978, I graduated from Towers High School and spent the next couple of weeks finalizing the plans for our wedding. Everything was coming together so beautifully, and I was so overwhelmed with joy.

Lisa in wedding gown

With the gifts from my bridal shower, I began moving the kitchen items (which consisted of glasses, dinnerware, flatware, Crock Pot, can opener, mixer, etc.) into our rented apartment. Setting up housekeeping was the most exciting time, putting everything into its place and decorating our first home. I had so much fun going over and "playing house" like any young bride-to-be.

June twenty-fourth was the big day. I couldn't believe it had finally arrived. We had a traditional church wedding with all the trimmings. My wedding gown was long with a three-foot train following behind, covered in layers of white lace. Brad was waiting for me at the altar in his tuxedo with tails. Bridesmaids, groomsmen, and a best man stood alongside. My father walked me down the aisle, kissed my cheek, entered the pulpit, and performed the wedding ceremony. My grandmother, Bert, was my matron of honor. At age eighty-one, she was nearly as excited as I was! The photographer took photos during the ceremony while everyone was facing the minister, but my grandmother turned her head to face the camera. I remember thinking how cute she looked. She was so honored when I asked her to be in my wedding. What a glorious day!

Brad and Lisa's wedding with matron of honor
Grandmother "Bert" facing the camera

After the wedding and reception, we left the church in our well-decorated Chevy Camaro. With tin cans streaming from the rear bumper, we were off for our honeymoon. We didn't have much money, and we thought we were going to our apartment for the night. To our surprise, Brad's father had purchased a local motel room for the evening. We spent the next day at Six Flags over Georgia screaming on the roller coasters and having a blast. A few days later, we returned to begin our life together. Everything was wonderful, and we were thrilled with our youthful newlywed life.

Brad and Lisa at wedding reception

I began working as a secretary with the Department of Natural Resources in Atlanta about a month after returning from our honeymoon. I enjoyed the job, the people I worked with, walking the streets of Atlanta during lunch, and seeing things I'd never seen or experienced. Remember that I was only seventeen at that time, so I was getting my first glimpse of the real world—and loving it!

As the summer stretched into fall, on September 2, I celebrated my eighteenth birthday. Another year older and growing as a couple, we were making our first memories and just enjoying life. As husband and wife, things couldn't have been better. All of our dreams were coming true.

My Life Changed Completely

*S*ometime in the middle of November (I can't recall the exact day), I went to work as usual. The morning tasks were normal; I answered the phone and typed. When it came time to break for lunch, Donna, my coworker and I made our way to one of our favorite spots to eat. We had a cafeteria upstairs in our building that we often frequented for our "breakfast of champions," which consisted of a Honeybun and an iced Coca-Cola. For lunch we enjoyed getting out for some fresh air. With autumn breezing through the towering skyscrapers, we walked a few blocks to the restaurant, entered, and ordered our food. The restaurant was always crowded, so we pressed through the rush of people and made our way to a table. We sat down and began to eat. Halfway through our lunch, I noticed my hands were trembling. I held them out across the table and showed them to Donna. I had no control over the shaking. Donna, shrugging her shoulders, passed it off and said we needed to finish up and get back to the office. I assumed that with her lack of great concern that I'd be okay and didn't really give it further thought.

We finished our meal and returned to work. Our office was small, occupied with three employees including myself. The room next door was a laboratory with ten or twelve technicians who tested water from different counties. Off to one side we had another room where the file cabinets were located next to the lab.

The doors to each room remained opened as we entered in and out, working together.

I had some invoices to put away, so upon returning from lunch I was standing in front of the file cabinets when all of a sudden my heart began to race. Pounding as if I'd run a marathon, a feeling of fluttering was rising up in my neck. My throat felt like it was closing up as if I were being smothered. The voices coming from the girls in the lab seemed to roar in my head, fading out as they reached my eardrums. I was unable to distinguish or make any sense of their vocabulary. I swallowed intensely, holding my neck, trying to stop the feeling, but it continued. Nothing seemed to work. In desperation, I ran to Donna, I was terrified. I thought I was dying. I begged her to help me as I struggled with all the scary sensations while the horrific thought screamed in my head: "This is it! You're dying!" My heart was racing, and I knew something was terribly wrong. It wouldn't stop. It wouldn't calm down. "Oh no, I'm dying! Don't let me die! Please don't let me die!" I clung to her, begging, pleading, "Don't let me die! Please, help me! Oh somebody, help me! Something is wrong!"

We had a nurse's station upstairs, so Donna advised me to take her arm and go there to get checked out. As I entered the elevator and felt the confinement of the doors closing behind me, it still didn't compare to the smothering feeling I was having as my breathing continued to struggle.

When we reached the nurse, she could see the horror in my face and ordered me to lie down. She checked my blood pressure and gave me a medication called Dramamine, which I now know is for motion sickness.

She asked me questions, "Do you have anything on your mind? Are you going through a crisis? How are things at home?"

I began searching desperately.

What could she mean? I have everything I've ever wanted. Everything I've ever dreamed.

The fear gripped me, and, unknowingly, I began my journey of panic attacks. The confusion and fear surged through me repeatedly. I'd feel my body trying to calm down, and then it would come again like a rushing wave flooding over me.

Terrified and panicked, I thought, *I must be dying.*

I believed that so much that I told Donna I loved her and hoped she believed in God because He's real and we're all going to die one day. The Bible says in Hebrews 9:27, "And as it is appointed unto men once to die." I know I have an appointment, but like the country song performed by Kenny Chesney expresses, "Everybody wants to go to heaven," but nobody wants to go now! I was fighting with everything in me to survive.

In a state of bewilderment, I spent the remainder of the day in the nurse's station. I never calmed down completely. Just a few hours seemed to last an eternity as I lay on that cot. After work, Donna met up with me and drove me home. We didn't say much on the ride. I was so confused and scared and just wanted to get home. I'm sure her mind was racing as well, but I don't recall any conversation as we traveled the thirty-minute-or-so commute.

When I arrived at home, relieved to be away from the office, I told Brad of the events of the day. He listened and looked at me puzzled. Of course he had no clue; neither of us knew what had happened or what lay ahead.

The next morning I went back to work at 7:00 a.m. Still confused, those feelings of fear and death seemed to roll into another day. Day after day I tried to continue my job; however, I found myself spending lots of time in the restroom trying to pull myself together. I recall hiding in the stall, praying for relief and clutching the Bible that I began to carry in my purse to work. It eventually got so bad that I couldn't keep my focus on my work, so I quit my job. I felt like such a failure, lost, not knowing how to put my life back together or how to fix things.

How can I stop this vicious spiraling?

Feelings of death consumed me. My dreams, my plans, and our newlywed life all turned into a nightmare, and it seemed that no matter what, I couldn't awaken. My life had changed completely.

Doctor, Doctor, and Dear Ol' Dad

I had headaches all through the fall of the year. I now know I have allergies, and ragweed was out at that time. So I was having headaches that worsened no matter what I did. Some days I thought my head would explode with the pounding. And then there were headaches that had the sensation of a vise tightening around my head. That is when I began my trips to the doctor. I just knew there had to be something wrong.

I've got to find out and get some help. If they would just put me through extensive testing surely they're going to find something, I just know it.

At times I remember thinking maybe I had a brain tumor, and they'd find it, remove it, and I'd be okay again. Not ever considering the seriousness, in desperation I just wanted so badly to find an answer, something the doctor could pluck away and bring me back to my old self.

I went to see a family physician that I later found out had been a military doctor. He had great respect for men, but he thought all women were neurotic and just a big walking bundle of hormones. My mom had an episode with this doctor, but she didn't tell me until years later. She had an allergic reaction to a new brand of dryer sheets and broke out with a rash all over her entire body. That doctor prescribed something for her nerves. Later, mom's friend asked if she had changed anything. Recalling the dryer sheets, she discontinued them and her rash diminished immediately.

The same doctor prescribed tranquilizers for me, an eighteen-year-old girl. There was no thorough exam; although, he did rub my forehead and tell me I had tension-itis, which is not even a real medical condition. He also prescribed another medication for the headaches. So Brad and I were off to the drug store with great hope of getting some relief. I refused to take the tranquilizers but filled the prescription for the headache medication. The drug knocked me out, and it took hours to wear off once I awoke. I could have coiled from my miserable existence and slept the world away, but I didn't want that. I wanted to be fixed. I loved life and wanted mine back. Who can function and solve problems if they're asleep or in a stupor from medication? That is when I realized: Unfortunately, there are doctors who will pack you full of pills, write you off, and send you on your way.

I've always, to my knowledge, been very healthy and haven't taken anything other than an occasional aspirin. But the headaches continued, the fear continued, and the confusion was enormous. The feelings of death kept haunting me, and I started to grow afraid of being alone. I was afraid I'd die and no one would be there to help. While Brad continued to work, God bless him, I began spending my days at my sisters' homes. Sometimes I would stay with my sister-in-law, Jackie. I just didn't want to be alone. Each night I'd desperately seek out where I'd be spending the next day, and Brad would drive me on his way out each morning. That was the most unsettling time in my life because no place gave comfort. Restless and dealing with a continuous feeling of fear, a churning stomach, rapid heartbeat, and shakiness, everyone was looking and wondering, "What is wrong with Lisa?"

I remember many nights, I sat straight up in our bed scared out of my mind.

"Brad! Help me! I feel like I'm going to die!"

My heart was pounding, my breathing was shallow, and horror

swept over my entire body. The Bible says in 1 John 4:18, "...fear hath torment." I know it was tormenting me.

"Brad, you've got to take me to my parent's house!"

For some reason I wanted to be there if I were dying, or maybe I thought my parents could rescue me. I just wanted to step through the doorway and feel the peace of home engulf me. I have no idea why, but Brad would always get out of bed and drive me. Many nights, we stood on my parent's front porch knocking on the door at 2:00 or 3:00 a.m.

Dear ol' Dad would open the door with his hair standing straight up on his head and say, "What's the matter?" Eventually he stopped asking that question because time after time of this a.m. knocking, my father knew what "was the matter". Like any other dad, I'm sure he grew very tired of it.

Looking back now I've wondered why he opened the door again and again, but he always did. The last time I knocked on his door crying, "Daddy, I'm dying. Please don't let me die! Make this stop."

I pleaded with the man I always thought was stronger than life itself. He glared at me in his frustration of being awaken night after night; I'll never forget when he asked me if I had a chronic illness.

"No," I gasped, laying my hand on my chest.

"Eighteen year old girls don't just die," he said.

As I looked into his face, I tried so hard to grab hold of his words and hyperventilated with each sentence coming from his lips. He proceeded to order me to lie down on the floor and just die.

That statement hit me like a ton of bricks. "What?" I asked. "I can't."

"Exactly. Go home and get some rest so the rest of us can do the same!"

In shock of what I was hearing, I looked at my father and I stood up. Brad and I left and returned home to some of the best sleep I'd had in so many nights. Unfortunately, my fear perched on the edge of my bed waiting for me to awaken the next morning.

The month of November and the beginning of December 1978 seemed to last an eternity. I was still so confused and felt as if my life was crumbling right before me. No one had any answers, and my parents couldn't fix me. Not even dear ol' Dad.

Parents: Vernon and Johnnie Smith

REAL LIFE CRISIS

Christmas was around the corner, and even among all my horrible feelings of fear, confusion, and now depression, Brad and I decorated our apartment to celebrate our first Christmas as husband and wife. We bought our tree at a roadside tree stand and shopped for all the trimmings at a store called Lionel Play-world. I put our names on our Christmas stockings with glitter and glue. We purchased green, blue, red, gold, and silver Christmas ornaments to hang on the tree. There were strings of silver bells wrapped around it and a beautiful white star shined as the topper. Icicles shimmered as the final decoration. It was our first tree, and it was so beautiful! It felt great to have some sense of normalcy.

Lisa decorating first Christmas stockings

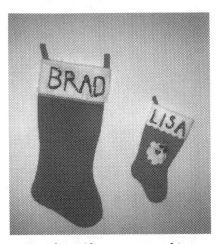

Our first Christmas stockings

On Christmas Eve, Brad and I decided to go to my parents for a visit—not in a state of panic, just a normal visit. On the ride over, a woman turned left in front of our car as we crossed a busy intersection. There was nothing I could do as Brad slammed on the brakes. I just tried to brace myself for what I knew was inevitable.

I remember the sound of the screeching tires as the skidding car slung us all around the seats—there wasn't a law for seatbelts back then. I saw the horrified face of a child as it came closer and closer, and our cars met on impact. I was thrown forward, my face hit the dashboard, and then I fell backward into my seat. I reached up and touched my lip as it began to bleed and swell instantly. Brad and I stumbled from out of our car, and he checked on the other driver and the child. More shaken than anything, it turned out that we all managed to be okay—just banged up and bruised. But our car was totaled; our only means of transportation was gone, and I didn't have a job.

Well, Merry Christmas, I thought as I stood there and stared at the crushed front-end of our Camaro.

Brad's mom, Anita, happened to drive up to the intersection minutes after our collision. Realizing she was seeing our crushed car, she frantically emerged from her car and ran to where she found us standing on the side of the road. Brad had called my parents, and they drove over to take us home from the accident. The police report was written, and the wrecker loaded up and hauled our car away.

We spent the holidays riding with relatives to the family gatherings. With blurred vision and terror sweeping over me as we rode in the backseat of my brother-in-law's car, we traveled up I-20. I remember asking him to slow down while the other cars on the expressway whizzed by. He laughed, and, while the radio blasted, he tried to assure me that he had it under control. When you've recently been in a car wreck, the last thing you want to do is speed up on the expressway—or any other road for that matter. Even though he gave me his assurance of his driving abilities, I definitely did not feel in control and hadn't for quite some time. That drive took an hour. Not once did we slow down, and everyone in the car seemed fine with the speed—everyone except me. After a shaky ride, we finally arrived at my father-in-law's home safe and sound.

In a room full of family, I felt so alone. My thoughts overwhelmed my whole being, and though I tried to concentrate on the events of the day, fear and anxiety separated me from the fellowship.

Lisa at Father-in-law's for first Christmas in the worst time of panic

Christmas had come and gone, and now we were facing another struggle. Brad had been working as a millwright since before we were married. His job consisted of traveling from one construction site to another as they completed the installation of conveyors. Now without any means of transportation, he received his pink slip. With no income left, we decided to give up our apartment before we were evicted. We packed boxes, but this time it was without the exhilaration we once felt as that soon-to-be newlywed couple. We paid for a storage rental with some of the last money we had. I remember gazing into the roll-up door as we stacked the fragments of our home one on top of the other. My brother, Steve, offered us a place to stay with him and his wife, Terri. The agreement was that we could live with them until their first baby was born, which Terri was expecting at the time. Brad found employment again at a company called Metro Carbonation, he road to and from work with our brother in law until we were able to purchase a used car. With the employment things seemed to be getting better financially.

We stayed in Steve and Terri's small spare bedroom and condensed our bed size to a single-sized bed. We were uncomfortable night after night but very grateful for the place. It just wasn't our home—the home we had tried to begin. Living in another woman's turf was also difficult. It was Terri's space, decorated with *her* special wedding gifts and such. I thought we got along well, and it all seemed to work out—until Terri went into premature labor. She delivered their son, Keith, two months early. Again we had to move. Thankfully another brother, David, and his wife, Jane, allowed us to live with them.

Brad borrowed the money from his dad for a deposit on our second apartment. We moved again into an all-adult community. Upstairs, on the third floor, I remember Brad and my brothers struggling to carry our bulky couch and other furniture items from one level to the next. They made each turn by maneuvering each piece over the wrought-iron handrails.

I began afresh to set up housekeeping in my world of anxiety. I tried to step out and meet other ladies in the complex. I made friends with one who was home during the day. I remember being invited to a fabric store to pick up materials for her beautiful hand-quilted blankets. I rode with her to the store in such a state of anxiety it felt as if I were in a dream. It seemed as if I bounced around like a ball in a pinball machine springing from one bumper to the next, only going through the motions of living.

Brad bought an older Ford Galaxy from a friend as our replacement car. I kept the car each day as he rode with his brother-in-law, Earl, to work. I was so nervous when I drove anywhere. There were times when I drove to my sister's, I was horrified when I looked through the windshield—I prayed for God to just get me there.

I became pregnant in April of 1979. This news brought some light into my world of turmoil. I loved children and had discussed many times with Brad of having at least two children, agreeing on three at the most. Brad's sister, Bridgett, found out she was also expecting. His grandmother, who we called Tuck, bought us matching maternity tops. Even though I wasn't showing at the time, I wore my new top as if I were huge. I was so excited about the baby; finally something positive was happening in my life again.

Two months into the pregnancy, I began having problems. My sister, Dondra, had experienced some of the same symptoms with her pregnancy, so I thought maybe it was okay. One afternoon, while shopping with another sister, Karen, I began cramping. I made an appointment and went in to see the doctor. He sent me home with instructions to take it easy and said I would be fine.

After speaking with Brad's father and his stepmom, Diane, they suggested that instead of climbing the three flights of stairs at our apartment, we should come and spend a week with them in Dallas, GA. Brad and I discussed it and decided to go. He continued to work in Atlanta during the day. My anxiety level was very high, but Diane helped by teaching me to sew. We had only been there a few days, and one morning after Brad had left for work, I started having horrible cramps. I pleaded with Diane to get me to the hospital as the pain worsened. She agreed and helped load me into the backseat of her car. She covered me with a blanket, closed the door, and hopped into the driver's seat. She began the long route by weaving through the back roads of Dallas until we reached the expressway in Douglasville, which finally led to the hospital in Atlanta.

When we arrived, the medical team took me back immediately, examined me, and said I was having a miscarriage. The doctor said he needed to perform a DNC and keep me overnight. After the procedure, groggy from the anesthesia, I was admitted to a room. I lay there listening to the trains of baby beds as they were being rolled down the hallway to the new moms so they could feed their babies. Now the babies stay in the room with their new mommies, but in those times they all stayed in the nursery down the hall. I can't imagine why I was placed on that hallway after having a miscarriage.

Oh, the crying you would hear as the nurses wheeled the babies into each room. I remember feeling the pain of not having a new little one to hold, and as the tears flowed down my cheeks, I covered my face with my pillow and tried to muffle out the sound of their cries.

Later that same evening, a nurse came in and asked me how my feeding went. I told her I had lost my baby. She held her clipboard to her face and apologized as she exited my room. I cried myself to sleep that night, and left the hospital the next morning. Alvin and Diane suggested that we return to their house until I fully recovered, but I just wanted to go home, lock myself inside, and shut out the world.

After being home a week, I received a call from the doctor's office informing me that I needed to follow up with another test. Brad drove me to the hospital downtown, and they expressed to me the concern of possibly having had a tubal pregnancy. They proceeded to do an ultrasound, and from the results told me I had a mass that needed to be evaluated. So into surgery I went a second time in less than two weeks. Upon waking in the hospital the next morning, I was assured everything was fine, no mass, I was then released to go home.

With the loss of our first baby and our world turned upside down, my fears continued to manifest. Depression truly set in. I recall sleeping to avoid the days. If I was asleep, I couldn't feel. I soon gave up driving due to feeling so out of control. I remember one final episode that convinced me to throw in the towel, not to mention the keys...

I was spending a great amount of time at my parents' house during the day while Brad worked. My mom expressed to me that they were going out of town and were leaving early in the morning. She asked if I could make a deposit for her at the bank. I assured her I would, and, feeling nervous when it came time to go, I asked my grandmother if she would ride with me. She told me to take my little brother along with me instead. Jason was probably five years old at that time. Off to the bank we went, only about six or seven miles away.

Feeling anxious, I made my way and my mom's deposit. During the ride home, I began to feel very scared. My vision blurred, my heart pounded, my breathing was shallow, and I felt out of sorts. All those same terrifying feelings overwhelmed me again. Nothing looked familiar as I continued the drive. Feeling lost, I pulled the car over into a nearby subdivision where I tried to calm down and gain a sense of control. I was disoriented because of the many turns that wove through, and I struggled to find the main road from which I had veered. I realized my brother, being so young, had no idea there was a problem. Although, for me, the fear magnified, and I knew he depended on me to get back to my grandmother. I drove in a daze, cloud-covered eyes, pounding heart, trembling hands, and begged God to get me back.

Finally the driveway was in sight. I pulled in, put the car in park, and got my little brother out. Shaken, as I stepped inside the house, I vomited. My grandmother couldn't begin to imagine what I'd experienced; all she understood were the words I shouted, "Never again! Oh my gosh! Never again! I will never drive again!" I imagined what could have happened if I wrecked the car and hurt my brother or someone else. Nothing could be worth that.

Feeling depressed, like a failure, after a miscarriage, with no job, and an old replacement car, I questioned over and over, *"Why, God? Why?"*

I pondered every moment, every struggle, as I watched my life disintegrate. We were building on a year and a half of unwanted memories. Recalling the words of the nurse during the onset of my first panic attack at the Department of Natural Resources, "Do you have a crisis in your life?"

Now I could truly say, "Yes! I'm in a real life crisis! *Now* would be the time for anxiety!"

It's Your Nerves

With new employment and a new apartment, the old feelings of fear remained. Still searching, I talked to everyone hoping someone had an answer—our minister, my family, our friends, anyone I could think of, anyone that would listen. The same answer echoed in my ears over and over as they all told me on different occasions, "Lisa, it's your nerves. Nerves. Nerves. Nerves!"

What did that mean? I'd heard of elderly people saying they had bad nerves. *I'm eighteen, how could I have bad nerves? What happened to my nerves? What caused them to go bad in the first place?* I was once the person who did everything, went everywhere, loved whizzing around in my car with the windows down, radio up, the wind blowing through my hair. And now shrinking from life- what had happened to me and that person I once knew?!

Please, God, help me find an answer to this nerve thing that has possessed my soul. I remember lying on our bed with my face buried in the pillow, pleading with God that I needed help so desperately.

A couple of evenings later, Brad and I were at the mall. I don't remember a reason for going shopping, but as we entered a bookstore I began reading the covers through the many racks until I came across a small paperback titled *Peace from Nervous Sufferings* written by Dr. Claire Weekes. *Isn't this what everyone had been saying—nerves?* I picked the book up and began to glance through it. To my amazement the words seemed to leap off the pages. The writings described everything I was going through. I didn't want to put it down; finally something, someone had some answers! I went immediately to Brad and asked if we could purchase the book. I read the pages to him with my eyes filling up with tears; he saw the relief I was receiving, and we bought the book. I had my nose in the book the entire ride home.

Glued to this book endlessly for hours, even days, but still believing in my King James, this book became my Bible. I clung to it like a child with its favorite teddy bear. I kept it in my purse and took it with me everywhere I went. I'd pull it out hoping to gain a sense of just what the title read, *Peace*. Many times when I became afraid, I would refer back to it. There were always chapters that spoke to me and explained the feelings of fear that gripped me to my core.

In my fog of bewilderment, I still didn't fully understand this road I was traveling, but with the help and information in this paperback, I knew I was having what Dr. Claire Weekes described as panic attacks. I tried so hard to gain as much knowledge to help me get through just the average day. For everyone else, life seemed to roll along, but for me a typical day consisted of blurred vision, everything seemed so out of focus, shallow breathing as though I were gasping for each breath, loss of appetite, no desire to sit down to a meal with my stomach churning with the gut wrenching turmoil that was going on inside, fear of death lurking constantly over me as if at any minute I would find myself falling out, fear of being alone with no-one to help pull me out of this horror, fear of being crazy and locked away, worry, wondering if those awful feelings would come again—only to wake up to them day after day.

I still tried to do the things I needed to do and take care of our home to the best of my ability; just trying to function on a daily basis became such a task. Different people gave their input of how and what I should do: get busy, learn to crotchet, invest in someone else's life, and forget about my troubles. There were threats from loved ones that warned I'd better get it together and be concerned about Brad reaching his limit and leaving me for someone else.

Boy, that all seemed like good advice, and even *I* have been guilty of giving such wisdom to others at times.

There were those that told me, spiritually speaking, that I had the "spirit of fear." Others frightened me even more with their input. I was almost convinced that I needed to be concerned about my furniture moving around the room and pictures floating off the walls. Once, I had a minister pray over me as if he were performing an exorcism. I had another friend request for me to read the book titled: *Fear, the Destructor.* Unfortunately, these things added to my fear, and the vicious cycle continued its downhill spin. I was so overwhelmed; it was unbearable! 1John 4:18 "There is no fear in love. But perfect love drives out fear, because fear hath torment." My weight dropped dramatically, and at that time it was weight I really couldn't afford to lose. My sister Leslie became very alarmed, and to this day reminds me of when my clothes hung on my too-thin frame.

PANIC, PREGNANCY, AND MOTHERHOOD

The new company Brad was working for needed help in the repackaging department. Brad was the supervisor over this department, and I had met the company owner who offered me the position. I accepted and moved into the work atmosphere where I no longer had days alone at home. With Brad as my supervisor, it all worked out very well in my favor. I could work and make an extra income for our family and still have the security of my husband (who knew what I was going through) at my fingertips.

The job was going well, and, believe it or not, a husband and wife can work together successfully—or maybe we just had to, simply for the demand of an extra income. We continued working from the end of spring through sometime in December 1979, and then I became pregnant for the second time. I was so sick during this pregnancy. Each day, going to work and just trying to hold my head up was a challenge. I'd heard of morning sickness, but this was all hours of the day. I remember the smell of the co-owner's cologne making me sick on several occasions. It really wasn't any one smell or food that I could put my finger on, just merely my body and this baby trying to adjust. At first I was worried about the new pregnancy; it had only been five months since my previous miscarriage. But after contacting the doctor, I was reassured. Time and time again of being so sick, and after vomiting in the middle of the warehouse floor, I was told that it would be in my best interest to take the time off. I was told that I could return to work after the birth of our baby. Excited again about becoming a new mother, I now began to focus on the baby growing inside.

The apartment complex that we were living in was an all-adult complex. With the money we'd received from the insurance company as a result of our car wreck, we had just enough for the down payment on a mobile home. Things began to look up, and that is when we moved to Henry County.

Five months into the pregnancy and in a new location, I was home alone again. I didn't know anyone. I was about twenty miles from my parents' home, Brad's work was thirty minutes or so away, and I had no means of transportation (even if I'd reached a point of bravery to drive anywhere). Still panic-stricken, I spent my days cleaning and taking care of our small home, which left me with a great amount of time on my hands. Looking out the window on those wintry, cloudy days, feeling like I was the only person in the world, I remember the times when panic would surge through me like electricity, so quickly flushing through my body as the flash of lightning surges across the sky during a stormy night after the heat of a long summer day. I saw, day by day, my mind and body working against me.

I soon met a neighbor, Darlene, who came to my home to sell cosmetics. She became one of my dear friends. I thank God, for she truly was heaven-sent. She was one of those people you meet for the first time and feel as if you've known your whole life. Very outgoing and fun to be with, she helped fill my days. Darlene was a mother of a two-year-old daughter. Since she had been through the experience of pregnancy, she had a lot of information to offer. Understanding that with panic attacks you tune in so intensely to what's going on in your body, the major introspection can be so alarming. I reflect back on a time when my anxiety was so severe: A cloud moved in front of the sun, which changed the lighting in the room—even *that* caused me to panic. I was so sensitized that I could not distinguish between what my body was doing and what factors were going on in my outside world. Darlene, unaware of my anxiety at the time, helped me to distinguish between panic and pregnancy.

We spent a great amount of time together, and eventually she began getting me out and about. We spent time at her home, which was only three doors up the street. I could only comfortably venture a few miles in the car with her to a store a short distance away having in my mind that if I needed to get home quickly we could get right back. During the summer that year, we attended a church VBS a few miles away, which was a milestone for me. Darlene was good company for me, and I'm thankful for the friendship that still remains.

Brad took me to the pre-natal checkups, and, for the most part, the pregnancy went well. June 21, 1980, our daughter, Alicia, was born. We were excited, young parents, as you can imagine any young new parents would've been. Returning home from my hospital stay, I was not only plagued again by fear and panic, but by the fear of being alone and panicking while responsible for our daughter. As I gazed into that little face that looked to me for her security, I wanted to be all she needed and more but felt so inadequate.

Lisa holding newborn daughter, Alicia

I thought motherhood would be something I could handle very well since I grew up in a large family with three younger siblings. I knew how to change diapers, feed and burp a baby; and without the panic, I'm sure everything would have been great. But I had an infant who was new to me and not to mention had acquired the colic. Alicia cried many hours of the day with a tummy ache, I could hold her, bounce her on a pillow in my lap, put her in a swing, but nothing soothed her. As she cried my anxiety soared and I am certain she felt my nervousness. Darlene was there in the beginning of my motherhood experience but unfortunately she moved away. I was left alone, again.

There were sweet times with my new baby, in spite of the panic. I relish in the memory of the aroma of the baby lotion just after a fresh bath and the cuddling and bonding of mine and Alicia's beginning relationship as mom and daughter. Each day, I'd watch her sleep, snuggled in my arms. I just regret the panic and anxiety that accompanied me and robbed me of the most precious time in my life—when I became a new mom.

From Panic to Phobia

One evening, Brad and I took our little one to visit his grandmother, Tuck. Bridgett was also visiting with her son. During our visit, she asked if I would like to ride with her to a store similar to Walmart. I agreed; we left our babies with Brad and Tuck and headed to the store. When we entered the building, we browsed around and looked at the clothes and the many different items. As we pushed our buggies from rack to rack, my vision did not seem clear. I felt like the bright, florescent lighting made the store look foggy, and it cast a haze covering throughout the store. I was bothered by it and felt as if I were in a dream-like state. I kept shopping and tried to get past the feelings that felt so strange.

Bridgett said she needed to go to the restroom, so we ventured to the back of the store where it was located. Waiting, standing at the sink, I felt panicky. I knew that panic was the name of what I was experiencing, but I still didn't understand anything about it. I was unaware of how to work through it, so my body began to fight against the feelings. Bridgett stepped out of the stall and asked, "Are you okay? You look like you've just seen a ghost!" I said to her in total fear, "You've got to get me out of here!" I was terrified and felt as if I couldn't breathe. I know you've heard the phrase "so scared you can't see straight." Well, that's exactly how it was. "I can't breathe! I can't see clearly!" I clutched my hand to my chest which felt as though I were being smothered; my heart raced and pounded as I said, "Please, get me out of here! Bridgett, I can't breathe, I can't see! Oh help me, get me out of here!"

Bridgett took me by the arm and led me out of the restroom and through the store. As we made our way, we passed other customers and headed toward the exit; my vision was completely blurred. I tried to focus on the people as they passed, but they appeared as only smudged objects. The exit seemed miles away, and I was horrified. I felt trapped, like I would never escape. When we finally exited the store, we found the car, and I climbed in. I was shaken and wanted desperately to get back to Brad.

That was the beginning of my avoidance pattern. I began to eliminate any situation where I'd feel anything of that sort. I'd get out quickly! I avoided outings to the grocery stores, malls, restaurants, or any public place where a repeat of the shopping experience with Bridgett might occur. Then I was housebound. The only place I continued to go was church on Sundays where I'd sit near the exit, never in the middle of the pew, always on the end seat, just in case. There were times in our church services that I left the sanctuary. At times I would stand outside the interior double-doors and peer through the small glass windows as I tried to listen through the barrier. I wanted to capture a portion of the pastor's message and hoped God would give me a word. I also continued to visit family; but I was very uncomfortable, and the visits were strained. A very limited space became my world. A prisoner in my own home, I had no idea of the phobia I was acquiring each time I avoided a situation. Venturing outside of our mobile home, just going to the mailbox, became a forced task. It seemed that my body swayed as I walked to pick up the mail at the end of the driveway. I became a prisoner and later realized I was the warden that held the keys to my self-made cell.

Agoraphobia—fear of the market place. The definition is much larger than that. It's actually the fear of any situation you feel you can't escape quickly in case of a panic attack. My whole existence became one big "What if?" What if I go into a store and that happens again? What if I can't get out next time? What if I panic while alone with Alicia? What if? What if? What if? You can't imagine the "what ifs" a mind can come up with when it's gone through such an ordeal. "What ifs" consumed my every waking thought.

Later I returned to work with Brad at the same company I worked before Alicia's birth. We placed her in daycare, and I worked for the next four and a half years. Working again helped with our finances but increased my dependency on Brad. I grew afraid for him to leave me, and he became my safe person should any situation arise and cause me to panic. This played havoc on our relationship many times, like when the daycare called to inform us that Alicia was sick and needed to be picked up. We'd both have to leave, pick her up, and we'd return to the workplace. I'd stay in the car outside the building and care for her because I knew Brad was just inside *if* I needed him.

What an enormous strain on our marriage, and what a great load on my husband. Neither of us had intended for any of this on the day we said, "I do." Life has a way of not always turning out like you planned. And surely this was something out of our control at the time.

There we were, still a family like any other family with the everyday necessities and needs such as groceries and diapers to be purchased. I didn't want to be left alone, yet I couldn't do the shopping. When Brad was in the grocery store, I stayed in the car. I feared panicking and not being able to reach him. I couldn't go into the store because of my fear, and cell phones didn't exist back then. I was afraid to be left alone, yet I couldn't go in.

What a dilemma! Fighting became the everyday norm. Any time a situation arose where Brad had to leave the house without me was a huge ordeal. Tempers flared. Sometimes objects flew across the room in the middle of the rage. Neither had the knowledge or support of how to handle what consumed us. We merely reacted. Brad was lost in how to handle things, and I clung to the only security I felt that I had left.

I did try to "get a grip," like others had mentioned. One time,

I spoke with the owner of our company about my fear of driving. He suggested I try to make the drive on my own to the daycare. He told me of someone he knew that overcame their problem of hyperventilation by pressing on and breathing into a paper bag. After our conversation, I tried to drive alone to pick up Alicia. It was a beautiful day, and the sun was radiant. But as I drove through the winding road and the sun flickered through the trees, I began to panic. I pulled over into a convenient store and called my sister-in-law, Jackie. She met me and followed me the remainder of the route. Brad got a ride with a friend and returned home later that afternoon.

We met a new couple that moved in next door, and we became friends. I opened up to the woman, Karen, and told her of my many fears. She was so interested that she read my book *Peace from Nervous Sufferings* by Dr. Claire Weekes. Karen became a great support during that time, and I confided in her often. With her help and understanding, I tried to face the panic head on.

One evening she convinced me to stay with her at home while Brad did some grocery shopping. I agreed, and I began to panic no sooner than he'd left the driveway. Karen helped by explaining what she'd read in my book and compared it to what I was feeling. She assured me that this wouldn't kill me, and I wouldn't lose my mind, which were huge fears of mine at that point. I sat on her couch in such a state of fear and tried to embrace everything she said.

My vision blurred, my heart raced, my hands were clammy and tingly—just like in the store with Bridgett. As I tried to consume Karen's information, the panic did seem to subside. I was amazed when my body started to calm down. Typically, I ran away from and fought those feelings. I usually coiled like an infant in a fetal position. But this time was different. Unaware while it was happening, it was the first time I faced the panic. The reassurance Karen was giving as she quoted inserts from the book was so soothing to my soul. She told me I was okay, the fear was only feelings that could not harm me. Sounds easy, but it was only the beginning.

During a panic attack, the body goes through so many physical changes. Vision blurs, hands tremble and tingle, breathing becomes shallow and rapid, the heart races, the digestive system goes haywire, legs feel like they won't hold you up, yet you feel you could run a marathon in order to escape it all. And your friends say, "Let's go shopping!" Do you understand the dread I felt when I was asked to go on those ventures?

I'll be Home for Mother's Day!

*M*y fears and agoraphobia continued for two years. I tried to speak to my family members about what I was experiencing and how I didn't feel like myself. I made the comment that I didn't know who I was anymore. I became the laughing stalk of my family. In such a large family, people will talk. One sister mocked, "Who am I?" She'd moan and aggravate me by saying that if I couldn't remember who I was, I should wear a nametag to recall my identity. Laughter would sore throughout the room. At many family gatherings, different people would zero in on me about my fears. "Are you afraid today?" "Do you think you're going to die?" Many nights I left gatherings in tears. In Brad's frustration, he'd say, "We won't go back." But they were my family, and I loved them. I wanted to go back. I don't think they meant harm, and sometimes people think making light of someone's situation is the correct thing to do. Without knowledge, people often look at a situation and try to analyze or give their opinions, which too many times are better left unsaid.

I grew up listening to all kinds of Elvis Presley's music, I love to hear his rendition during the Christmas season of the song: "I'll be home for Christmas." However, it wasn't Christmas at all. Mother's Day was around the corner, and my mom requested in lieu of a gift that she wanted her eleven children to come home for Mother's Day. She asked us to spend the night without spouses or grandchildren. I was still totally dependent upon Brad, so I worried sick over this as Mother's Day drew closer. I love my mom, and I wouldn't have wanted to deprive her of her gift, but I also knew she wouldn't understand where I was in my life.

Mother's Day, Grandmother Bert and Lisa's Mom, Johnnie

On numerous occasions Brad and I talked about the upcoming event, and he assured me that it would be fine. When the time came, Brad took a pillow and slept in the car outside my parent's home just so I could attend my mom's "Mother's Day gift."

We were all scattered around the living room, in sleeping bags, on the couch, or curled up in chairs. We stayed up all hours of the night and reminisced of our childhood days. Everything seemed to work out well. I was there for my mom, and Brad was secretly just outside, so my fears never manifested.

I made it through the night, and it all seemed okay, until the next morning when two of my sisters, Dondra and Karen, woke up before me and caught a glimpse of Brad outside the window. Outraged, my sister, Dondra, began pointing her finger at me, "Lisa, I can't believe you put Brad through this and made him sleep in the car all night! What is *wrong* with you?! How could you do that to him?" I begged her not to tell everyone, and I tried to explain to her that she just didn't understand what I was going through.

Praying no one heard her, I tried to quiet her down. I was so embarrassed and felt enormous guilt, as you can imagine, but so phobic I couldn't rise above the situation. Dondra finally calmed down, but I spent the remainder of the morning worrying that when the perfect time came, she'd tell it all.

Everyone had breakfast around the table. The family was all together, still laughing and recollecting old times, enjoying each memory, and having a great morning. As my stomach churned after each bite, I'd glance across the table at Dondra. *Is she going to tell? Will she embarrass me once more?* Fortunately, as we finished our breakfast and cleaned the last dish, my sisters gave *me* a gift that day: They didn't expose me or my secret. And as for my mom's gift, I was home for Mother's Day!

But because of the ridicule and embarrassment I began to hide my feelings. How could I explain something I didn't fully understand myself?! So it became my secret. I kept it hidden from the rest of the world, especially my family.

COUNSELORS

One Sunday afternoon, Dondra and her husband, Rick, invited Brad and I to go out to eat. Still hiding my phobia, I decided to go but planned to sit near the exit just in case I felt the need to escape. This had worked well for me on several occasions in the past, so each time I'd request to sit by the exit. But this time I had no control. As we entered the restaurant, the hostess asked, "How many?" and proceeded to seat us in the back of the restaurant, away from the exit. I started to follow everyone, but the farther I went the more anxious I became, so I turned around and went out the entrance door.

I made my way to our car and stepped inside. Waiting, I didn't know how I would explain this one and still keep my secret. I hoped Brad would soon make excuses and come out so we could go home. Instead, after a few minutes, Dondra joined me in the car. She asked me what was wrong. She said she could understand if I were crippled or had something wrong with me in that aspect, but she didn't understand why I couldn't go sit down in a restaurant and eat. She asked what was going on with me, and then she insisted I'd better seek some help.

Isn't that what I'd been trying to do? I had spoken with ministers, friends, and family. At one point, I even went to a county mental health center where I had a panic attack in the woman's office. She had instructed me to come to a session of group therapy, which I did. I'll never forget that day.

Brad walked me into the building down a long hallway. He said he'd be back in an hour or so. As I entered the group therapy room, a woman took my hand and said I could partner with her. As my eyes scanned around the room, I began to focus on the many people with terrifying physical handicaps. My fear magnified. There were people seated in wheelchairs, drooling with their heads hung to one side, moaning out sounds. With each pound of my heartbeat, my mind screamed, *Run!* I pulled my hand from that woman's, and with every muscle in my legs, I ran as fast as I could down that long hallway and out the exit door. Hoping Brad had not left, I saw him in the distance and shouted, "Brad, wait!" He turned and saw me running toward him. When I reached him I cried, "Thank God, you hadn't left! Get me out of here!"

I couldn't see the similarity of my need and those that were in that building. I never returned. I had also met with a psychologist who said maybe I'd lost my identity after I told him I didn't feel like my old self. I saw him a few times and then gave up on him too. I knew from the book *Peace from Nervous Sufferings* that I had panic attacks, and I was struggling with agoraphobia. I also knew that I was frustrated with the help I'd sought, yet I realized I couldn't conquer this one on my own.

When I returned home from the restaurant on that Sunday afternoon, I searched through the yellow pages, which at that time was like today's "google". I called a crisis hotline, and the woman on the other end instructed me to call my county counseling center. Early Monday morning, I made that call and was put in touch with the director, Debra Davis Brown. I explained to her what I'd been going through, but since I already had several failed attempts in trying to receive the correct help, I asked her to tell me the meaning of agoraphobia. It might sound like an unusual request, but I had been through enough. Debra gave me the definition and then continued to explain that she would counsel with me but said it was my decision to make the appointment. I expressed to her that my phobia was so great that I was unable to meet with her inside the building. She offered to meet me outside.

I made the appointment, and in the cold month of February, Debra greeted me and Brad with three chairs outside the building. That was the beginning point of weeding through my life and what had happened to bring me to this place-trying to understand anxiety, how it had affected me, and discovering why I retracted from it. The bewilderment of how this had happened kept me questioning. The fear engulfed me and became a vicious cycle. Living in what seemed to be a fog, I tried to grasp the information I received from Debra. It was horrendous.

One afternoon while counseling with Debra, still continuing our sessions outside, she pointed to a box of tissue sitting in one of the office windowsills. She instructed me to go inside the back door into the office to retrieve the tissue box and return it to her. She told me exactly which office door would get me to the destination. I'll never forget that trip, for it was the beginning of my many steps inside that building, many steps into battling agoraphobia. Feeling excited and scared all at the same time, I walked to the back door of the building. I turned the doorknob and stepped inside, made my way to the first intersection, and turned left. My heart pounded as I walked past two offices and into the third office, where I saw the tissue box. I scooped it into my hand and quickly made my way out of the building.

As Debra diligently worked with me week after week, she even rode in the car with me in order to get me back behind the wheel. One afternoon as we worked on driving during our conversation Debra enlightened me that she loved tap dance. I have always enjoyed dancing, watching musicals, etc. When Debra realized my interest she invited me to take a dance class of jazz and tap that she instructed. I was very excited to take the class but very anxious at the same time. Brad agreed to take me to dance and Debra who knew of my agoraphobia/panic was there so I thought everything would be fine. I believe she used this as another exposure therapy in getting me out there. I took the class and loved every minute. I was even in dance recitals on stage with my heart racing like no one else. I knew every exit and I reminded myself at any point I could just leave.

Debra worked on exposure to the fear as she assigned more homework, which consisted of staying home alone to deal with the physical feelings of fear on my own. In another assignment, she had Brad and I go to the grocery store and enter the entrance, then immediately exit. At that point, stepping inside the grocery store made my fear so great that everything past two or three feet in front of me was completely blurred. She repeatedly stressed the importance of practice. It was a long road ahead; but I was making tiny steps of progress, and it felt great.

Debra was truly a God send and I am so thankful the Lord not only led me to a knowledgeable counselor but to a life- long friend.

> Proverbs 12:15 "The way of a fool is right in his own eyes, But a wise man is he who listens to counsel."
>
> Proverbs 11:14 "Where there is no guidance the people fall, but in abundance of counselors there is victory."
>
> Proverbs 13:10 "Through insolence comes nothing but strife, but wisdom is with those who receive counsel."
>
> Proverbs 24:6 "For by wise guidance you will wage war, And in abundance of counselors there is victory."

We continued working to overcome the phobia by putting me in situations that created panic and trying to make me realize I wouldn't die, nor would it drive me to insanity. The panic was still very frightening, as were the sensations, and the "what ifs" that clouded my thinking. I felt as though I had to walk through the fire. "Panic until panic no longer frightens you," Debra said. But so many times it was easier said than done! I had not learned the skills of coping with panic; I just kept panicking and tried to convince myself that through it all I would be okay. It was the most difficult thing I'd ever battled. I continued, and I trudged on.

Brad, Lisa & counselor Debra.

BRAD CHANGED CAREERS

*B*rad had taken the Civil Service test in 1980, and now, three years later, we were arriving home from working at Metro Carbonation. With our usual routine of the day, we checked the mailbox. Brad flipped through the envelopes and saw the letter from the Postal Service, opened it, and read that they wanted him to come in for an interview. As soon as he read it to me I began to worry. *I can't stay at home for any length of time alone without panic*, I thought. Yes, I was practicing and doing my homework Debra had assigned, but I was still very frightened, still not quite grasping the acceptance of the panic.

Brad was excited about the invitation for the interview. It was a great opportunity for him and an increase in pay, which would be good for our finances. Everything seemed to start going in that direction so quickly. Brad spoke with his parents, and his grandfather gave him a tie for the interview. His whole focus became the Postal Service. I felt so removed from the elation everyone else was feeling. I was afraid, and it didn't take long for anger to set in. I felt abandoned.

In counseling with Debra we informed her of the upcoming interview, and she seemed very excited for Brad; this too made me angry. Not only did I feel he was leaving me high and dry, but now she seemed to be deserting me also. I'll never forget the day she was praising Brad and then turned to me and said, "Lisa, Brad has figured out what he's going to do with his life. What are you going to do with yours?" Those words angered me all the more as they echoed through my head like cymbals clanging together with a horrific bang.

I once knew what I had wanted with my life. I wanted to get married, raise a family, grow old with my husband, and live "happily ever after." But my plans changed when I was sideswiped with panic and agoraphobia. It haunted me endlessly. I left that counseling session so mad I could have screamed. I remember slamming the car door as I got in the passenger seat to go home. As the anger bellied up I resented the panic and agoraphobia. I felt cheated, cheated of my dreams.

Debra continued to assign homework, and now with Brad's upcoming career change we worked on my being home alone. At first my time consisted of small intervals of fifteen minutes, which continued until the time increased. Eventually, I conquered the fear of being home alone. Brad's interview went well, and he got the job with the Postal Service.

Alicia was now three years old staying at home with Mom. Karen, my neighbor and friend, who was also home during the day; and I spent time together as our daughters played. Still suffering with agoraphobia, our visits were limited to our homes and backyards. Our friendship continued to grow, as did our girls, and now, with our income increasing, Brad, Jimmy, Karen, and I began looking at new homes in our area. We enjoyed our friendship and decided we'd like to build new homes together and remain neighbors. We bought lots and worked with the builder in completing our house plans.

With the excitement, Karen and I spent time together going through samples picking out wallpaper, paint, flooring, etc. Each day I began riding with her to the construction site, which was only a few miles away. We were anxious to see the progression of our new homes as they began to take shape. In September 1984 they were completed, and, as Brad worked at the post office, Karen and

I began moving our smaller boxes with great anticipation. The blessing of moving into a new home and moving from a mobile home into our first house was a wonderful time, and, even more so, our friends were making the move with us.

In November I seemed to get more control of my agoraphobia, so Karen and I ventured out and did some Christmas shopping. I still avoided shopping malls and larger stores, so we shopped in small-town villages. Even though I was enjoying this new feeling of freedom, anxiety was ever present.

Christmas in our first house–Brad, Lisa and Alicia

All the changes with Brad's new employment and our new home turned out well. Alicia soon began kindergarten, which was another adjustment for me. I had grown accustomed to the noise of the girls playing, and I struggled to release her as the bus left my sight. Closing the door behind, the silence seemed unbearable as my focus turned inward. I'd turn on the TV for company and go about my routine of cleaning the house and doing laundry. Some days were fine, and I'd get caught up in the work while the time seemed to quickly pass. Other days would drag along as the anxiety mounted.

School brought plays, field days, and other activities. I wanted desperately to get involved and be the mother Alicia needed. Brad and I would attend the school programs and sit by the exits. I remember one field day we watched all the events; then, Alicia's class returned inside to their classroom for their refreshments and their end of the year party. I was fine outside during the relay games, but when they headed down the hallways I turned and remained outside. Brad went to the party without me.

I felt I had made progress and felt good about the accomplishments but still had that wall I couldn't seem to hurdle. I would step out only to recoil when I'd feel the escalating panic; then I'd stop in my tracks. It felt like a wall. I could go only so far, and I'd feel like an invisible wall popped up pressing against me, preventing me from taking just one step farther. The voice inside my head would say "just go" but I would retreat back.

Time Moves On

*A*s I'm writing this, I'm thinking of events that have leaped yet into another year. Let me just say life continued to happen; time moved on. The clock never stops whether life is on the mountaintop or if you're in the valley. There were rainy, dark, cold, dreary days and days of glorious sunshine. There were usual days with school, church, family activities and outings just like everyone else. Still trying to face the fears that had kept me in bondage in times past, I continued to make improvements. I met other women and became friends with about six ladies in my area. Living in the same neighborhood and attending the same church made our friendships easy to maintain since they remained in my realm of things. Even though my world was expanding, it was still small and contained. I felt comfortable enough to venture out with some of my friends since they knew my condition, and if I began to feel panicky they'd return home at my request. We built a trust, and my girlfriends were great.

Without trying to contribute to my fears, my friend Laura talked me into going to the mall one evening. She assured me that she knew every exit. "Girlfriend, I know that mall like the back of my hand," she said. Her plans were to walk into the food court, go a few steps through the mall, and exit. She wanted to practice and encourage me. We entered just as she had said, and, with my anxiety high, we made our way through the food court, into the mall, and walked to the exit. Laura assured me that she had taken the same exit in times past. It was actually a service entrance for store deliveries that lead to hallways on the outskirts of each shop. When we entered the hallway to the exit, the double doors were barred with chains and pad locks. Instantly, I felt trapped and began to panic.

For some reason we never considered turning around and going back the same way we came, but in such a state of panic it wouldn't have mattered either way. We just kept pushing through the service hallways of the mall. Concrete floors, block walls, and florescent lighting engulfed us as we wound through like rats in a maze. We searched for a way out as I held tightly to Laura's arm. With my usual blurred vision, we desperately turned up one hallway and down another only to find dead-ends. Winding and weaving through, I felt I couldn't breathe. With my heart pounding, we rounded one more corner and my eyes zoomed in on the wide swung opened doors, my nose was drawn to the smell of the night air that led to my escape. So frightened and yet so relieved, I pressed my back against the Macy's exterior wall and slid down to my knees. Shaken, Laura and I began to laugh and thank God we had found an exit. To this very day when we recall that incident, we laugh as Laura mocks the word I screamed that night, "Laura!" A fond memory we share with great laughter, but, unfortunately, it added another "what if" to my list: *What if the doors are locked and I can't get out?* So I continued to avoid.

Lisa and Laura

I've had many people ridicule me through the years for having this phobia. I had people I trusted that tried to force me through the panic. I've been in situations riding in the car with others that took complete control of the circumstances and kept me against my will. These events only added to my fears. For those of you trying to help someone with the struggle of panic attacks and agoraphobia, thinking you can force them to overcome is completely ineffective. I lost confidence in those people and became hesitant to travel with others.

In our Fairview community there were shops about a mile or two from our subdivision. We had gotten to know one of the small town grocery store owners, Johnny. While picking up some groceries, he expressed that he needed some help in his store. He asked if I would be interested in working the following day with his wife. He knew we had only one car and offered to pick me up for work. With a mixture of emotions, fear and excitement, I asked him if I could discuss it with Brad and give him a call later that same evening. He agreed, and Brad and I went home to talk it over. I think Brad was surprised that I was interested in the first place, and even I was surprised at myself that I'd mustered up the courage to say yes to Johnny. I called him and agreed to help out. He said his wife would pick me up the next morning at 10:00 a.m. Anxiously, I saw Brad off to work and Alicia to school, and then I got myself ready.

I worked at the store for an eight-hour shift. Everything went well for the most part. I kept my fears at bay and enjoyed the day. At the end of the evening, Johnny asked if I could come in again the next morning. This continued until I was working three to four days a week. I had a part-time job and loved it. My confidence began to expand as did my world. I met so many new people in the area. Brad even fixed up an old truck he'd been storing away so I could drive our good car the distance of one mile to the store. I drove by myself to and from work every shift. We arranged for the school bus to drop Alicia at the store after school, and she'd remain with me until Brad returned home each day. His schedule was early in, early off, so our arrangement worked out great. I worked 10:00 a.m. to 6:00 p.m. about four days a week.

I did have panic attacks several times while working but found ways to hide it from my coworkers. In the afternoons, the store would fill up with customers stopping in to purchase bread and milk on their way home from work. Sometimes the anxiety would mount, but somehow I managed to run the register and keep them happy. I remember times when my line filled up, and I'd gaze at the customers through blurred vision, but I'd still fill their bags and send them on their way as if nothing was wrong.

I enjoyed my days off while at home; I kept up with my house-cleaning and laundry. I like having a clean home with everything organized; although, the time off from the store without practice made returning to work after a couple of days very difficult. One morning feeling old fears rearing up, I called one of my friends, and she talked me through the avoidance of wanting to stay home. I faced the fear and went into the store, which I know now was in my best interest. We are such creatures of habit, and the avoidance had definitely become a learned habit.

With business always changing, Johnny needed someone for a nightshift. When asked about the schedule change I refused it. I wanted to be at home with my family at nights. I worked at Johnny's for two years, and the job ended.

One of my friends, Judy, lived in my subdivision and had opened a hairdresser's shop in her home. She asked me if I'd be interested in helping out a few days a week. I had enjoyed working, and it always felt good to get out and be around people, so I accepted the offer. The convenience was nice; I could walk to her home if Brad ever needed the car. Her daughter and Alicia were friends, so the bus would drop them off at Judy's, and they'd play together in the house or in the fenced backyard. I worked at the shop for two years until Judy moved away, which again resulted in me being home.

While another year was coming to a close, my grandmother, Bert, fell and broke her hip. She was ninety-two years of age and still lived in the home with my parents. She had moved in with them after my mom gave birth to my eldest brother, Mike, in 1950. Bert helped with the children, the housekeeping, laundry, and cooking (I recall the homemade biscuits!). She loved flowers and working in her garden. She was like a second mother to my brothers, my sisters, and me. Everyone loved her because of her unique ways. She loved with all her heart and wouldn't think twice about correcting you if the need ever arose. But Bert never understood my panic and agoraphobia; how could I explain to someone who in my eyes had always been so strong and independent? She had raised my mom all alone without the help of her husband, who was murdered while she was pregnant. Bert knew hard times but pushed through them with every ounce of strength she had. She never owned anything of any material value, but she treasured my ten siblings and me.

During her hospital stay, my brothers and sisters took turns staying with her to relieve my parents. Because of the agoraphobia, I had not been on an elevator in years and couldn't go above the first floor without severe panic; remember I didn't venture far from the exits. I wanted so badly to be with my grandmother and felt guilty for not helping out. At the end of the week I spoke with Brad about going to the hospital and trying to see her. We drove over, and went inside where I walked to the elevator. Just the thought of stepping inside made me feel like I couldn't breathe. I stood there for the longest time battling within myself. Brad decided to go on ahead and find where Bert's room was located so he could report back to me and see if this was something I thought I could accomplish. He went up, but soon the elevator door opened back up, and my sister, Linda, stepped out. She seemed excited to see me and pleaded with me to hold her hand. She assured me that she'd help me get to Bert's room. Oh, how my heart was so heavy, but the wall of fear was so great. Reluctantly, I said, "I can't." Soon Linda gave up and returned on the elevator alone to go back to Bert's room. Again the elevator door opened, and, to my surprise, Brad was pushing a wheelchair with Bert seated in it and Linda following alongside. My eyes filled with tears, and at the same time I burst into laughter, for my grandmother was wearing a pair of plastic glasses with a huge nose attached as if she were ready for trick-or-treating on Halloween. I dropped to my knees and threw my arms around her; the joy of that moment I'll always cherish! We visited together for a while, and later they wheeled her back upstairs.

Bert was released from the hospital, and for the next two months, my brothers, sisters, and I shared the responsibility with my parents of caring for her. In December, we were all gathered for Christmas sharing in the food and fellowship that makes family time wonderful. We watched the children as they opened their gifts, never imagining that in just three days the lights of the Christmas tree would be replaced with the lights of an ambulance escorting my grandmother's body to the emergency room. Brad was working that morning; and when given the news that things weren't looking well, he came home, and we drove to the hospital where Bert still remained in the emergency room. We were instructed that she was just beyond the double doors a few feet away. Brad and I went in and I held her hand and kissed her cheek, telling her that I loved her. They soon moved her precious body to a room upstairs on the eighth floor. The day turned into evening, she took a turn for the worst. As Brad and I sat downstairs in the waiting room, family members came in and out giving us an update on how she was doing. One of my sister-in-law's expressions will be an everlasting image burned into the depth of my mind. When the elevator door opened and Jane stepped out, I knew by the look on her face without ever uttering a word that my grandmother, Bert, was gone. December 28, 1990, my sweet grandmother went home to be with Jesus. Oh, how my heart ached.

We all helped my mom with the funeral arrangements. We made the funeral home visits, and I did better than I ever expected. I was anxious, but the panic never surfaced. Bert was buried the weekend of New Year's.

Each New Year's Eve for quite some time, our family gathered at my brother, Roger's, home. All the ladies would unite in the kitchen "rattling the pots and pans" as my father would say. We rolled out homemade biscuits, fried sausage, bacon, and scrambled eggs. The children played and ran in and out of the house. The teenagers congregated out in the front yard, waiting to fire off their bottle rockets and any other fireworks they could get their hands on. But that year, the sadness in the house was overwhelming. Not all came, but for the ones that did we had our traditional breakfast and in our grief brought in the New Year. As always, time moves on.

Power over Panic (POP)

I continued to read everything I could find about panic attacks and agoraphobia. Friends would call and tell me of talk shows that were covering the subject. Anything I could gain, I soaked up like a sponge. I kept praying for a better understanding and hoped that something would click in order to conquer this ruling fear.

In 1991 I received information about a support group called "POP" (Power Over Panic). I contacted them and requested to be put on their mailing list. I received newsletters and learned about people with similar stories. It was great to have the support of others who understood what I was going through. I was invited to a POP meeting at the Hyatt Hotel in Atlanta. Excited about getting more information about my phobia, Brad and I decided to attend. Unfortunately, when we arrived at the hotel we found that the meeting was upstairs. I couldn't believe it! *Why would they host a meeting for agoraphobics upstairs?* I thought. Brad went up to find the location of the meeting while I waited downstairs, because I was still terrified to get on elevators or of going upstairs through hallways away from the exit. I still avoided them like the plague, and I was so aggravated because I had looked forward to this night. Brad came down and went back up a second time trying like crazy to find a way for me to attend. On his way down the last time he returned with the founder of POP, Marilynn Foster, a recovered phobic. She tried to convince me to go upstairs. She assured me that I could move around and exit at any time I felt the need. She said the doors would always be opened during the meeting. I was frustrated and kept thinking: *"How will I be able to concentrate on the things being taught when I will be so focused on my panic?" I can't just snap out of it, not even for this meeting.* Then, to my delight, Brad had found an exterior stairway that led to the entrance/exit of the conference room. We went outside and around the building to the stairway that led us to the meeting. Brad assured me that the door would always open and remain unlocked if I needed to exit. I felt secure and knew that when the meeting ended I could leave the same way I entered.

The meeting was wonderful. Stephen W. Garber, PhD, Director of the Behavioral Institute of Atlanta spoke and explained the fight or flight mechanism that God instilled in all people. It allows mankind, when in danger, to either fight or flee from what is perceived as danger. With the onset of my first panic attack and the fear of another one occurring, I had been fleeing an awful lot. The best news I received at that meeting was that it was possible to overcome my phobia! At the end of the meeting I purchased a workbook and video titled "Overcoming Fears, Phobias, Panic, and Anxiety." Returning home I eagerly watched the video and thought, *I'm going to make it. I can overcome this fear!*

I shared my new information with family and friends. My brother-in-law's mother, Louise, had also suffered with panic attacks and agoraphobia. I told her about what I had learned at the meeting, and she was so excited for me and told me she had confidence that I'd make it. She had suffered for thirty something years but never had the correct information to help her overcome. Each time we were together we shared stories as our phobic bond connected our souls. She expressed that at times with her panic attacks she felt as if she'd come to the edge of a cliff and was hanging on by a thread. She continued to encourage and cheer me on; maybe her hopes were to see someone overcome what had bound her for so many years. Louise has passed away, but I'll always hold dear to my heart her stories, her experiences, and her constant love and support.

Robin, a dear friend, was also a great support to me. She watched my video and even spent an hour of every Saturday morning to follow me in her car around my neighborhood in order to try to get me back on the road. This homework continued for several weeks, but, swamped by my "what ifs," I gave up. Driving alone has been one of the hardest fears to conquer.

Later in 1992, POP began a support group on the south side of Atlanta that I attended. It was really interesting to find out that I wasn't as unique as I thought. During one of the sessions, a phobic woman explained her trips to the mall. She talked about how she'd enter one major store and then exit and drive to the other end of the mall to enter another major store. This kept her from having to walk the entirety of the mall. I couldn't believe my ears! She was describing my shopping experience and my method of avoiding the feeling of being trapped on the inside of the mall. It was funny how we were so similar in our avoidance patterns, and realizing that gave me a sense of normalcy.

David Rush, PhD, lead the POP support group, and I began individual counseling sessions with him in 1993. David worked with me on a breathing technique and explained that the shallow breathing during an episode of anxiety is what caused my vision to blur. We also worked on driving where he provided me a destination to drive, and he'd soon follow behind; then we'd return to the office. Brad and I met David at the mall, and he worked to get me to go farther in without fleeing from a panic attack. Many early mornings we were there with the "mall walkers." While they exercised physically, I tried to trudge through my exercises of facing the fear. David always expressed to me that my thinking was incorrect and the "what ifs" that I'd conjure up were never going to happen. "Remember your breathing technique, and let's walk through this mall," he said. I recall the times I made it farther and the victory I'd feel. It was the best feeling to get through the fear. On one occasion I walked farther and began to panic. My first instinct was to flee, but David stopped me in my tracks and encouraged me to sit on a nearby bench until the panic subsided. I wanted with everything in me to run; but I sat there, and the panic reached twenty on a scale of one to ten. When it started to decline, it felt so good having stayed in the moment and come out on the other side of panic. "Peace is on the other side of panic." Practice made the difference, and the intervals without practice made it harder to get back "on the horse." With the therapy I was receiving with David, Brad and I began practicing things on our own. During trips to the grocery store I'd practice going farther into the store unlike times past. Brad was such a great support. Sometimes he'd go one aisle over and throw toilet paper or paper towels (whatever was unbreakable) at me, making a game of my practice. We laughed and gained ground at the same time. After making grocery shopping a routine, it became easier. While shopping one evening, a friend saw me in the back of the store and said, "Look at you, girl, way back in the meat section." I was making great progress and was thrilled. I imagined overcoming the phobia entirely. *Could I really have "power over panic?"*

Robin

STATISTICS ON PANIC DISORDER

*T*hese are some stats I found from Psychology Today I thought would be enlightening.

Definition: illness characterized by spontaneous episodes of intense, gripping terror accompanied by heart palpitations, dizziness, and smothering sensations.

Causes: psychological vulnerabilities, stress, unresolved childhood issues, heart conditions.

Length of typical panic attack: 10 minutes.

Typical frequency of panic attacks: four attacks over four weeks or one or more attacks followed by a month of fearful anticipation of more attacks.

Number of PD patients who also suffer agoraphobia: a fear of any situation which help or escape is difficult or impossible: 1 in 3

Percentage of PD patients who suffer depression as well: 40%

Number of Americans who experience panic-attack symptoms per month: 1 million

Number of Americans who will suffer from PD at some point in their lives: 3 million (or 1 in 75)

Aged 18-34: 37% Aged 35-64: 60%

Average age of onset: 24

Female to male ratio: 72-28%

Percentage who are unable to drive farther than three miles from their home: 50%

Percentage who abuse alcohol: 30%; drugs: 17%; tranquilizers: 42%

Percentage whose work quality declines: 83%; who lose jobs or income: 67%; who are unable to work for at least one month: 43%

Percentage who have attempted suicide: 20%

Percentage who are financially dependent on welfare or disability: 27%

Percentage of patients that treatment helps significantly: 70-90%

Most common treatment is behavioral treatment: gradual exposure to simulated panic situations (desensitization)

After researching on my own I found that 25% of patients that enter the emergency room thinking they have a life threatening issue were diagnosed with panic attacks.

CELEBRITIES WITH PANIC

$\mathcal{S}$o many times I have reminded myself and others that I have known that suffered from panic attacks and anxiety, we did not invent this. There are many and many more to come that have and will suffer panic attacks. The following is a list of celebrities that have been some of those that panic has struck their lives as well.

Amanda Seyfried	Howard Stern
Aretha Franklin	James Garner
Bert Reynolds	John Candy
Caitlyn Jenner	John Mayer
Carley Simon	Johnathan Knight
Cher	Kim Basinger
Colton Haynes	Lena Dunham
Dick Clark	Michael Jackson
Donny Osmond	Naomi Judd
Ellie Gouding	Nicole Kidman
Emma Stone	Paula Deen
Eric Clapton	Ray Charles
Goldie Hawn	Winona Ryder

I remember in those days of thinking that I was the only person in the world that had experienced this awful thing. No my friend, we did not invent panic...

Mitral Valve Prolapse: Still Phobic

I suffered from allergy headaches for years and was diagnosed with ocular migraines in 1991. The first time I experienced one of these headaches, I was reading when suddenly half of the page disappeared. The vision aura was followed by a headache. Concerned because I had eye surgery when I was four years old, I decided to see an ophthalmologist who performed several tests and concluded I was having ocular migraines.

I was instructed at the onset of the vision aura to take something for the possible upcoming headache and informed that sometimes the aura itself is the migraine. However, it was frightening to lose partial vision, and a few times I lost my vision completely. But I accepted the diagnoses, and when it occurred I took something for the headache and waited for my vision to return to normal. Most times I lay down and tried to sleep it off. My mom suggested keeping a food diary and record menstrual cycles as well. I followed her instructions to find there seem to be no rhyme or reason for the cause of the headaches. The migraines continued, and I actually still suffer from them. They were always consistent in their pattern until one afternoon I went to softball practice with Brad. I was sitting on the bleachers when another woman sat down beside me, and we began to talk. To my surprise, this was a girl I had graduated with from high school. We were questioning each other about our lives and what had gone on since school. Then at one point in the conversation I couldn't speak correctly. I knew what I was trying to say, but my speech was scrambled. In my own mind I questioned if I was nervous and tried to speak slowly, but I had no control over this confusion. Embarrassed, we both laughed; I thought I was tongue-tied and tried to pass it off until I stopped trying to speak at all. I can't imagine what she must have thought as she left, but thankfully my speech returned to normal. When practice was over, Brad and I left the field, and I told him what had happened. On the ride home I had another ocular migraine.

A few months passed, and I'd kept journaling the headaches, trying to see if maybe there was a pattern or if I had missed something. One morning I had another episode and found myself going numb in my face and hand. I called our family doctor who said she'd call in something for the migraine. I was alarmed because the migraine had never gone this route before, so I called a friend who's a nurse. I explained to her what had happened at the ball field, and she said I should make an appointment with a neurologist. I called a hospital to get a referral, which led me to Dr. Koenig, a neurologist in Riverdale, GA. When I called his office they had a cancellation and said they could see me that same morning. I got in touch with Brad at work, and he came home to take me to the appointment.

When we arrived at Dr. Koenig's office, I had to fill out the usual first-time patient paperwork and was called in to see the doctor. Dr. Koenig began questioning what had brought me there to see him. I had taken my journal and began telling him of the different events. He listened and took notes for several minutes, which led him in the direction of wanting to run some tests. A CT scan, EEG, and an EKG would rule out some of his concerns. He asked if I ever had palpitations or panic attacks. He proceeded to tell me that he was asking these questions for a reason and that he'd explain later. We went ahead with the test, and I was thankful everything was in his building on the first floor. The CT scan was painless; the EEG was also, but it felt strange with wires hooked to my head with goop in my hair while a technician viewed me through a window. The last test of the day was an EKG looking at my heart.

I was escorted back to Dr. Koenig's office and assured the test results were good. He prescribed an aspirin a day for the rest of my life used as a blood thinner. He said he wanted to request an echocardiogram and instructed that I call the office for the results on the following Friday. He spoke of a condition called "mitral valve prolapse" and of how I fit the physical profile. He also said his wife had this heart condition. Brad took me for the echocardiogram, which took a little time, but I was calm and comfortable with the tech who performed the test.

Thursday, the next morning, Dr. Koenig's office called and informed me that after he had gone over my chart again he was concerned about the numbness and speech impairment that happened at the softball practice game and wanted to send me to a lab for blood work. This was the only doctor I'd ever gone to who seemed to be so thorough. My mind was racing wondering if he'd find what he was looking for but at the same time thankful he wasn't writing me off. My sister Karen drove me to the lab where they drew the blood, and we later returned home. On Friday I called Dr. Koenig's receptionist for the results of the blood work, and they explained to me they would not have them for another week. The doctor spoke to me over the phone and began to tell me I have mitral valve prolapse. He informed me this condition causes panic attacks in some patients. "Could this have caused my first panic attack?" I asked. He answered, "Yes." Sixteen long years of panic and agoraphobia, bewilderment, and fear became a vicious cycle and took over my life.

With this diagnosis I cried feeling a sense of relief. Finally, some concrete answers! I was not grateful that I have a heart condition, but I felt God gave me knowledge. I had prayed for so many years for an answer. What happened to that young woman that lived a life with the wind blowing in her hair as she drove with the windows down on the car? At this time I felt the sweetest peace come over me. A burden, a weight had truly been lifted. Matthew

11:28 "Come to me, all you who are weary and burdened, and I will give you rest."(NIV)

Here's a little information about mitral valve prolapse quoted from a book titled *The Female Heart* by Marianne J. Legato, M.D., and Carol Coleman.

It is a congenital heart defect; it runs in families. MVP develops sometime during the fifth to eighth week of fetal development. MVP is an abnormality in the valve that guards the opening between the atrium, the left chamber of the heart, and the ventricle, the left lower chamber. The mitral valve consists of two flaps or leaflets that are anchored by guide wires to tiny, strong buttons or nubbins of muscle called papillary muscles. When the blood leaves the atrium, it flows through the mitral valve into the left ventricle. If everything is working properly, when the ventricle contracts the mitral valve should snap shut tightly and smoothly to prevent blood from seeping back into the atrium.

In MVP, for some reason, the valve leaflets become enlarged and misshapen, billowing like sails full of wind back up into the left atrium when the ventricle contracts. Instead of closing smoothly, they allow blood to leak backward into the atrium. It is the regurgitation of blood back into the atrium that causes the distinctive murmur of this disorder. About half of all prolapsed patients complain of heart palpitations or skipped beats. Some complain of panic and anxiety attacks thinking they may be dying!

On Friday evening Brad and I went to Alicia's high school homecoming football game. With Alicia in the marching band, we made friends with the other parents, and one of the mother's had mentioned on occasion that she had a heart condition. When we arrived at the game I saw Deniece and asked her about her heart condition. She told me she had mitral valve prolapse. I told her of my diagnosis also with mitral valve prolapse. She looked directly at me and said, "Honey, you'll think you're dying!"

In 1994 I would have ended my book with that last line. I thought that with the glorious knowledge I had received about the mitral valve prolapse being the culprit of my panic and anxiety that I would have moved right along in life.

So I spoke with my psychologist, David Rush, informing him I wouldn't be coming back nor would I meet him at the mall. He told me he was glad that I was medically okay but assured me that I still had a phobia to overcome. I hated that phone call with everything in me, and I felt he just didn't have any idea the weight that had been lifted from my shoulders. But to my disappointment, he was right. I had received some answers, but it didn't stop the panic when facing situations I had avoided for so many years. Again my quest continued, and my fight goes on to kick this phobia to the curb.

I've learned so much through the years in this battle, and as my first counselor, Debra Brown, once said, "Lisa, you may go ten years or more without panic, and then one day again it'll creep it's ugly head; but if you learned the coping skills for the battle, the panic will be like an annoying headache that you *can* readily dismiss." It is essential that you are taught how to cope with the panic. The panic is what I feared, all the horrible feelings, but if you take the sting out of panic you can alleviate it all together.

SELF-ESTEEM

*T*o me this phase in my book is so crucial. Through the years of anxiety, panic, and agoraphobia, I don't think anything has suffered as greatly as my self-esteem. Because of the overwhelming toll panic takes on your entire being, there is no question about why it ravishes your self-confidence. I felt like such a failure the day I walked away from my job with the Department of Natural Resources in Atlanta. And while I watch friends retire at this stage in life, with regret I look back realizing the retirement plan I could've possibly had these thirty years later.

I held down several jobs over the years that consisted of lower paid positions so that I could remain in my agoraphobic comfort zone. This too led to low self-esteem. I witnessed others around me, friends and family alike, soar ahead in careers/jobs, as I stood in the shadows with nothing to expand on but the life of an agoraphobic, never feeling like I quite measured up.

I watched other mothers spending precious time with their daughters shopping together, going to the movies and having mother/daughter outings, participating as school "room-mothers." I love my daughter with everything in me, but I felt like I failed as a mother. I was always on the "outskirts" of Alicia's life as I sat in the isle-seats, trying to be a part looking on from a distance.

I was a wife and companion to Brad; I struggled often with an inward battle that I failed him. I encountered other wives helping support their family households. They drove the kids to the doctor, school, dance classes, church functions, as well as grocery shopping. I wanted desperately to help Brad pull the load that oft times seemed to overshadow him. I wondered so often why he remained in our relationship with so many independent women that could've fulfilled his needs. Again I felt lacking.

As a friend, the relationships I held were those that came to my turf. I never drove to meet them for lunch, shopping, or a movie. If we walked together they came to me and exercised in my tiny existence. *Why do they continue?* I'd think. There are millions of people in the world to befriend.

As a daughter myself, I felt I failed the times I could have helped my parents with my aging grandmother in her last days. I struggled with guilt and instilled inward beatings telling myself that I didn't measure up to the abilities of everyone else. My brother, Roger, was diagnosed with cancer. In the last weeks of his life I was privileged to be able to spend a great deal of time with him. He never understood my agoraphobia. One afternoon my associate pastor, Brother Dee, came to visit Roger during his illness, and, while we sat on his front porch, Roger began telling Brother Dee how much he thought of Brad and, laughing, continued in assuring that he couldn't have put up with me all these years. At first I thought "typical brother" is going to aggravate his little sister in front of company and then he proceeded to tell how I had a perfectly good car sitting in the driveway, yet Brad had to drive me everywhere. My humiliation climaxed and struggling with the fact Roger was revealing my "secret" I wanted to melt and run off the porch that day.

At my church, I grew in many areas and felt comfortable helping in leadership positions—teaching Sunday school classes, holding the position of treasurer, leading Finance Committee meetings, facilitating Beth Moore Bible studies and Dave Ramsey's "Financial Peace," helping direct VBS. These positions have helped my self-esteem; realizing even with panic and agoraphobia, I do have talents and abilities to offer.

To my knowledge no one attending my church knew of my

"secret." Brother Dee had no idea what Roger was talking about; although, I'm sure he pondered the comment. I was so embarrassed and beat myself up almost the remainder of the day. I hated myself for the disability as though I invited panic and agoraphobia into my existence. I cried to my sister, Karen, over the phone, and she, with sweet compassion, tried to convince me to hold my head up and gain some sense of self-worth. Roger found out later how upset I was and expressed to me that he loved me and never intended to cause me hurt. Through my tears I think he caught a glimpse of the havoc the panic and agoraphobia has and does play on my self-esteem. Roger went home to be with the Lord November 1, 2009. I love him and miss him greatly.

Unfortunately, there are still other people who don't understand and would never put their nose to a book such as this. I've come to accept that there will always be people on this earth that just plain don't care. I had one man express to me he considered me to be dead weight on Brad's hands. With the lack of support from folks of that nature and the self-lashings I gave continuously, can anyone fathom why my self-esteem would go lacking?

An insert of Dr. Claire Weekes' letters to agoraphobics in the State Wide Agoraphobia Group I wish to quote here:

Probably what is needed most is encouragement. When a person says that for many years she has felt guilty and can't rid herself of this feeling, she should understand that others who have suffered as she has have rid themselves of feelings of guilt. Agoraphobia should not make the sufferer feel guilty, but I know how difficult it is for him to be convinced of this. There is a way to gradually loose the feeling of undeserved guilt. The sufferer puts behind the feeling of guilt; another different feeling will form, which will in time, replace the guilty feeling. Let me explain in this way. A young girl went through a very tough grueling time. She had recovered and began to study to become a social worker. She has written, "How glad I am that I know what it is all about! I can go up to a patient now, from my own experience speak his language and what is more, he would know that I understand. *My suffering was a privilege!* So beside any feeling of guilt, not one of you need worry about being "a weakling, etc." because many now know you are no weakling but have a lot of courage and in time, even the guilt will be pushed aside, to pride in knowing that you understand a condition that *so few understand correctly.*

DIAGNOSES & ANXIETY

I have found that with the self-esteem issue that so often accompanies anxiety I haven't always stood my ground in situations that I needed. Don't allow doctors or anyone else to make you feel you are crazy when you know something is going on with you and you are trying to get a true diagnoses and not written off as a patient merely suffering with anxiety.

I love my front porch and when we were building our house I remember telling Brad that I wanted a big front porch. He accepted my request and built a huge front porch onto our house. One evening I spotted some spider webs in the corner of the porch and decided to get the broom and swoop them down. I never considered protecting my eyes with safety glasses, I just went for the broom. After a couple of sweeps something hit me in the eye and I couldn't open it.

I had Brad check to see if he could see anything in it but he could not. I went into the house and tried flushing my eye with water. Nothing worked. Blinking profusely with tears running down my face we got into the car and drove to the Urgent Care in our area. After checking in they took me back and put a solution in my eyes that illuminated with a blue/purple color to show any foreign object in my eye.

The Doctor on duty said he saw something and began removing the debri. We returned home and I felt relief but the next morning

I could still feel something remained in my eye. I made a call to my Ophthalmologist who agreed to see me that same day. When he checked my eye he said he did not see anything in it. I left his office and again felt something was still there.

The next morning after being miserable through the night I went back to his office where he checked my eye again.

This Ophthalmologist knew I had written a book on anxiety and actually had received a copy of the book when it was first released. When he proceeded to examine my eyes a second time he seemed very frustrated with me and even firmly gripped my chin looking into my eyes as he said: "There is nothing in your eye." And then there was a pause as silence filled the examining room, as he began apologizing and said: "Oh wait, I see something."

At that moment I felt relief but at the same time I wanted to cry because of the harshness I felt in his voice and his hands as he examined me. Unfortunately, so many are mistreated as though you can't reason between a legitimate concern and your anxiety.

If I haven't learned anything else during my journey, I have learned to stand up for myself. When I hurt, I say I hurt, when I need help, I request help. I will speak up and will not be abused or mistreated again. Stand your ground, appreciate who you are. Anxiety does not lessen or define you. You experience anxiety. You are not anxiety.

Blood Pressure & Anxiety

*B*rad and I had planned to run some errands one Saturday morning. I woke up with a headache and took Excedrin migraine hoping to get some relief. After taking the over the counter medicine and resting for thirty minutes or so we were on our way. Excedrin migraine contains acetaminophen(Tylenol), aspirin and caffeine. Caffeine is a culprit that a person prone to panic attacks really should avoid.

We continued our day and ended up picking up a few things at the grocery store. When I was standing in the checkout line, my heart rate went up. Brad had already left the store while I was paying for my groceries. I finished paying and went outside to the car and told him how I felt. I didn't feel panicky or anything like that but that my heart took off in the check-out line.

Now that I am getting older I have to take that into consideration when dismissing everything for anxiety. I expressed that concern to Brad so we decided to get my blood pressure checked at the nearest Fire Department.

The EMT came out to the car and checked my pressure and by this time I did feel my anxiety rising. He said my blood pressure was high and that if I were his wife he would have me in the emergency room. Well, this really put me in a high state of anxiousness so we took off to the hospital. The medical team immediately took me back and began the normal testing for heart issues, etc.

Five hours later everything checked out fine. Anxiety! The Excedrin migraine containing the caffeine elevated the blood pressure, raised my heart rate and anxiety level. Then after the EMT scared me further everything escalated.

After this event every time I went to the doctor or even at my dentist office where they check your blood pressure, mine was up. I became worried over this and started becoming phobic about it, thinking "what if it is up?" and guess what the results were? It was up every time.

I have never had bad blood pressure readings in my life. As a matter of fact my blood pressure has always ran on the low side. I began taking it at home but again I could feel myself becoming anxious when I took the cuff from the bag. The readings were always elevated. Finally, I sought out my friend/counselor and asked for her advice. She told me to repeatedly take my blood pressure every day. Again a type of exposure therapy, do this until I no longer feared the "cuff".

I now take my blood pressure at home and the readings are excellent as they were all my life. I've never had high blood pressure just fear again rearing its head in another area. My body reacting to those fearful thoughts.

The method is the same when we think the worse, adding fear and "what if's" our bodies react to those negative thoughts. Changing the way we think is one of the greatest keys to overcoming this thing called "panic".

Philippians 4:6&7 "Be anxious for nothing, but in everything by prayer and supplication, with thanksgiving, let your request be made known to God. And the peace of God, which transcends all understanding, will guard your hearts and your minds in Christ Jesus."

GRIEF AND ANXIETY

*S*ince the writing and release of my first book: "Looking for an Exit" We purchased land with family and very close friends. The excitement of having our own "commune" as some would refer to it had wonderful privileges. We enjoyed our time together visiting, sharing in meals, cookouts, and riding our golf carts around the land in the crisp air of autumn as the colors of gold, yellow, red and orange exploded throughout the land. Walking in the quiet cold snow with my Mom as she threw snowballs at me. Precious times I thought would never end until the snowball of death began and let me say I don't exaggerate as the lives began to come to an end. I have experienced the grief of eight loss loved ones and the anxiety that accompanies it. The emptiness and the void that surrounds as I ride by my brother's house and see that strangers have taken up residence, passing my parent's home and having only the memory of my Dad sitting on the front porch.

How do we deal with our loss? Time passes and you would think you would be over it but there is no set time or date where the pain stops. Then you begin to fear the future. The anxiousness builds as you question: "What will become of me and my spouse?" "Who will go first? Who will get sick, diseased?" You begin to fear the doctor's office, if I don't go I won't be diagnosed with some dreaded. But life is still happening all around. Work, kids, grandkids. How do you continue a normal existence?

I sat on the porch swing with Brad on a beautiful night in February, unseasonably warm. Feeling the breeze as the swing moved to & fro. I felt the presence of his arm around my shoulder. An intimacy that otherwise would have felt safe and serene. As I turned my head and gazed across the front lawn my eyes viewed the light of the lamppost in my parent's yard. And then the reminder "they're gone", our times together as a family, traditions; the times of walking up just to visit and say hello, they're gone. The lump in my throat and the hole in my gut is ever present. Grief, I'm grieving. When does this leave? How long does it last?

You move into another moment, another day of routine and things seem to go along. You feel okay for that time and space. Then you see a photo or hear a song and again the tears well up in your eyes. Sometimes you can push it away and other times you find yourself closing yourself in a room so you can let it all out. You feel better for a moment and even say: "It is okay, I'm better and I'm getting past the pain."

You set your schedule for the week with work, church, grandkids, and chores at home. All the aspects of life that surround you every day. You get busy and things go on as normal until you walk into the store and there it is, the bottle of "Jergens" lotion and you recall the aroma when your Mom rubbed it on her hands. Again the reality sets in; she's gone. Sooner than you realized then you are standing at the graveside of your Father, another one gone.

Anxiety during grief is no different, the physical feelings are the same. My heart races, I fear the unknown. I find myself worrying over the "what if's". What if's turn into catastrophic thoughts which can lead to panic attacks. But you cope as you did any other time with the feelings. Remember they are only feelings that can't harm you. If anxiety is the normal way you handle things then even in times of grief you may experience anxious moments. It is okay, go with the feelings and know your heart races, your breathing is rapid, your thoughts run. Work on changing the thoughts, the "what if's", the negatives that are feeding the fear and anxiety.

In the process hold precious the memories of those you've lost, cry when you feel like crying, laugh when you remember the funny times and just grieve…

"He will wipe every tear from their eyes. There will be no more death or mourning or crying or pain, for the old order of things has passed away." Revelation 21:4

STAGES

I didn't want to leave my readers pondering the question: "Where is she now in her phobia? What has she accomplished; what has she overcome? What chains still remain?" So here I'd like to shed some light on where I am in this stage of my life.

With everything life has brought, I've learned there are stages and degrees. During my brother's cancer I was taught he went through stages in his illness. We all go through stages in our lives: childhood, adolescence, etc. I've also learned there are five stages of grief that we all face when we lose someone to death. We go through shock, guilt, anger, suffering, and recovery, sometimes repeating those stages over and over until our hearts finally heal.

Agoraphobia is no different; it also has degrees. In my late teens and early twenties I found myself in the very worse stages. I became so housebound, my space so limited. Then with the *correct* counseling in my late twenties and early thirties I overcame and ventured out more, working and loving the life I'd regained. My late thirties and early forties I found myself even less dependent. Brad worked many hours consisting some weeks of fifty or sixty hours. I was home comfortably alone days and nights. I'm able to do the grocery shopping and can shop in the stores alone. Now in my fifties, shopping for clothes and eating out have definitely become something I love and enjoy. We have a group of family and friends that eat out every couple of months trying new restaurants together. We go to all kinds of events for our grandchildren. I am usually completely comfortable at those events. We have joined a church that seats fourteen hundred that has two services where I am consistently intermingling with many people. I am at present just finishing up facilitating a ladies Bible study at my church. God has definitely grown this woman.

The greatest chain that binds is driving my car alone. I've accomplished driving with Brad as my passenger and more recent have driven several miles alone but still working on conquering this one.

This has been the biggest obstacle throughout this phobia, and I know that once I overcome this one, my freedom will be enormous.

Alicia and Lisa in Florida

Agoraphobia and panic attacks are no respecter of events or vacations. In times past they robbed the pleasure of the constant breeze blowing through my hair with the blue sky overlooking the ocean as the waves billowed against the sand. It stole the mystery of the mountains as we wound through the heights of the many curves winding it seemed endlessly through the hills. The many beauties God has given us to take time out from work and enjoy Agoraphobia overshadowed.

In recent years, we have enjoyed trips to the mountains, gazed at the magnificent splendor of the leaves in the fall of the year, and hiked up the trails to capture a glimpse of the rushing water falling over the rocks.

Brad and Lisa, trip to the Mountains

Vacations have been strained through the years. We traveled several times to the beach and to the mountains. I love both. More recent I have traveled to the beach again with some anxiety present but nothing compared to the victory I felt when I stuck my feet in the ocean after so many years.

Lisa's recent trip to the Ocean

I have overcome many obstacles. I press on and pray God continues to bless me in my efforts to move forward. I'm sure I am blowing the minds of many of my acquaintances that had no idea of my limitations with agoraphobia/panic attacks. I never in a million years would have imagined writing this book and exposing myself in such a manner. In Beth Moore's Bible study she writes: "One of the most important parts of fulfilling our destiny is transparency." I can't get more transparent than this. Beth Moore also said, "You can't amputate your history from your destiny. Your history and your future are the same root. Learn from your history—*there is treasure there.*"

Panic and agoraphobia have been my history. This has been my life, my portion.

"I was not called to an easy life. I was called to a purposeful life"

"To serve God is to serve others. And to serve others is to serve purpose (Beth Moore).

FROM THE TRAILER TO THE DWARF HOUSE

*C*hanges, stages, another change in my life has come since the writings of my first book: "Looking for an Exit". Brad had his own business for twenty years and as of February 2015 the Lord again changed our path. It is always amazing to watch where God leads. The people He brings into our lives and the ones that come only for a brief moment.

God is constantly working to complete His plan for our lives and it is my prayer that I don't miss what He has for me to finish while I'm here on this earth. "For I know the plans I have for you, declares the Lord, plans to prosper you and not to harm you, plans to give you a hope and a future." Jeremiah 29:11.

In 2015 a Team of Dwarf House & Truett's Grill Operators came together to discuss hiring Brad as their Facilities Director. (The Chick-fil-A Dwarf House is a unique restaurant that sets itself apart from every other regular Chick-fil-A store. The Dwarf House, founded by Truett Cathy, is a modern day version of Truett's Dwarf Grill in Hapeville, Georgia, which was founded in 1946. Truett's Grill opened in 1996 to celebrate Truett Cathy's 50th anniversary as a restaurant owner.) Brad has worked in these stores since 1999 and let me say he knows each one like the back of his hand.

Upon much discussion and prayer the Operators hired Brad and guess who they hired as his Administrator? You guessed it! Me. God has truly shown His love towards our family and continues to grow me in my everyday experiences. The same twenty year old that stood gazing out a kitchen window in my mobile home stricken with panic is the same woman God has placed in the Dwarf House & Truett's Grill Restaurants working with others in sometimes very crowded stores.

Greeting others with a smile on my face and enjoying the people God allows me to work with each day has been wonderful. God has brought me this far and I am so excited to see what He has next!

Lisa working @the Chick-fil-A Dwarf House

Puzzle Pieces

*I*n my walk with panic and agoraphobia, I think back to the experiences, and I marvel at the beginning and the steps I've taken to reach the point I've attained. Puzzle pieces are truly what I've found. With each new form of information I've stumbled upon I've added another piece to my puzzle board. It's been an enormous ride, let me just say.

I'd like to list here those pieces in an order as they fell into my life and then give some instruction on how I've found they worked for me.

Puzzle Piece One: You won't die from a panic attack.
Puzzle Piece Two: You won't go crazy from a panic attack.
Puzzle Piece Three: Stop adding a second fear or what-ifs.
Puzzle Piece Four: Breathe from the gut.
Puzzle Piece Five: Practice makes perfect.
Puzzle Piece Six: The greatest of all: God Almighty.

Puzzle Piece One:
You won't die from a panic attack.

Dr. Claire Weekes wrote the book *Peace from Nervous Sufferings*. It was through her writings I found puzzle piece one. Doctor Claire Weekes spent thirty years in practice—first as a general practitioner, then as a physician, and finally as a consultant physician with special interest in the anxiety field. Dr. Claire Weekes spent eighteen years completely involved in the treatment of agoraphobia in the United Kingdom, United States, and Australia. She is the bestselling author of four books, and in 1981 she wrote her fifth book. She believes agoraphobia has wider implications than just open spaces. The incapacitating fear away from safety of home, particularly isolated or crowded places or anywhere the sufferer cannot make a quick escape or get help should their fears, as thought, grow beyond them. It includes the fear of traveling, especially a vehicle that cannot stop at will. Agoraphobia is one of the worst phobias; in view of all this, its notorious intractability, the success Dr. Weekes has had by remote direction through her books and recordings is truly remarkable.

I thank God for her education and willingness to help people with this struggle. I've questioned, "Was this her God given destiny?" We all touch the life of another just like the pebble making ripples in the pond. She touched my life. She wrote time and again that despite the severity of the panic you feel, you can't die from it. Dying never comes from a panic attack. Of all the thoughts I've had over these years with panic attacks, the very first thought that gripped me to my core was the thought: *I was dying.* I knew for certain *"this was it"* during my first panic attack. And time and again when panic reared its head I grasped onto the people around me, pleading with them to prevent me from dying. In my early stage of panic, I had one experience with my sister, Dondra, and her husband, Rick. We were visiting at their home when panic flooded me with all the horrible sensations. I reached out to Rick, a very laid-back guy; he kind of laughed in amusement that he couldn't save me if I were truly dying. We all have an appointment, but I've learned that panic attacks are not my exit. You could say that it was the immature mind of an eighteen year old but even older people who've suffered with panic attacks also recoiled in fear awaiting their "assumed" death.

PUZZLE PIECE TWO:
YOU WON'T GO CRAZY FROM A PANIC ATTACK.

wThis horror kept me bound in a cycle of fear. Oh, the times I thought for sure I was losing my mind. How could I not with so many haunting thoughts that plagued my head every day? Life took on a whole new phase once panic and agoraphobia became the new me. The "what ifs" that raced through my waking thoughts kept me *feeling* crazy. And with friends and family that were just as ignorant to the subject as I was, I'm sure they thought as well I was "losing it."

The times through blurred vision I saw the world unlike I'd ever seen before. Nothing made sense in trying to piece my life back together. I stayed in a state of bewilderment, asking myself, *Why, what, how, and what was possibly coming next?* There was always the fear of what lay ahead down this road I was traveling uncontrollably. A letter from Dr. Claire Weekes to the State Wide Agoraphobia Group:

I have found that many think they will pick up new symptoms. It may comfort you to know that the action of adrenalin is always restricted to the same organs and so must follow the same pattern. *There are no more surprises for you.* This thought comforts most people because apprehension of what can happen next. If you had only some of the symptoms mentioned, do not immediately think you must experience all the others. It is unusual to have all the symptoms. Each of us has some parts of his/her body more sensitive than the rest, and which therefore react more readily to stimulation by adrenalin. If you had not been nauseated or have not vomited, it is because your stomach is strong enough to withstand tension. It should continue to do so. We all know that certain people have a tendency to "heave" when upset, others run to the toilet, while others just churn inwardly. Few do all three. Your particular pattern has probably declared itself by now, so you can be comforted by the thought that you have experienced the worst.

The days that I felt normal were so often short lived trying to raise Alicia and be the wife Brad needed and that I wanted so desperately to be. Living out the daily schedules and routine with the physical feelings of shakiness in a constant state of general anxiety left me with one thought: *I'm losing my mind!*

The one time I reflect back to is the day I was home alone when we first moved to Henry County. I was experiencing panic attacks regularly and had a small understanding of panic. I struggled daily fighting sometimes, it seemed, for my very survival, and, as I write, my mind can see clearly the kitchen window as I stood gazing out washing dishes when panic whirled through me once more. My thought was, *I'm losing my mind, going* crazy *for certain!* Then in a state of desperation I spoke aloud, "It's the same feeling as when you thought you were dying!" I was learning for the first time that the feelings I had when I thought I was dying felt exactly as the feeling I was having when I thought I was losing my mind. *It's panic; you're not going crazy.*

The suggestibility that comes with the anxiety is unbelievable also. Anything I would hear about an insane person or television shows or movies of that nature brought horror. My eldest brother, Mike, also a pastor, came by my home one afternoon. He'd been to a nursing home visiting an elderly lady from his congregation. He was telling me she had no idea she was even in the world as a result of Alzheimer's. Unaware of the meaning of Alzheimer's, after my visit with Mike that day I began the "what ifs." *What if my mind ends up like that?* Again, another obsessive thought to bring on panic. I just knew I was like whoever the unstable person was. So often I imagined myself being locked away in a padded cell never to be returned to society again. Who wouldn't have had that thought when your world spun out of control and nothing or no one I knew gave any hope for my future. Terrified, I was thinking panic would reach an all-time high taking me away with the thought of an insane asylum looming constantly in the depth of my mind.

Again referring to one of Dr. Claire Weekes's letters to an

agoraphobic reader, she writes to the State Wide Agoraphobic Group:

As you know my patients are afraid of going hysterical, *a fear they've never done.* Action is different from thought; *you are not going mad!* There is nothing peculiar about you because you feel this way, it is still *not madness,* has nothing to do with madness.

PUZZLE PIECE THREE:
STOP ADDING A SECOND FEAR OR WHAT-IFS.

Where do I begin with this one? My battle with my thoughts has kept the agoraphobia alive, and I've learned changing the thought process is where I'll eventually find victory. When the initial panic attack occurred, my mind began to race, and still to this very day I have to counteract and reprogram. Your thoughts can run away, and sometimes it seems you have no control. I laugh at my husband, Brad, when he refers to this as "brain vomit." But I thought it is such a good example because at times my thoughts did just that—rolled vomiting one into the next, keeping the cycle of fear alive. It seemed sometimes to come from nowhere. But I've learned I'm the one that's adding and allowing them.

The "what ifs" truly consumed! *What if I die? What if I panic while I'm alone and no one is there to help? What if I go crazy and they lock me away forever? What if I panic and the panic never ceases to come? What if I panic in front of my friends that are unaware of my phobia? What if I run crazy through the mall panicking? What if I panic and crash my car hurting myself or someone else? What if Brad dies and I'm all alone to function? What if people find out about my panic and agoraphobia and don't want to continue our relationship leaving me to feel like a fool?*

Dr. Claire Weekes spoke of a "first and second fear." Your "first fear" is the feeling, and then we add a "second fear" with our thoughts. For example: My heart begins to flutter; then, tuning in, my thought added becomes, *Oh my, What's wrong with me?* The heart fluttering could be a number of things: too much caffeine, mitral valve prolapse, etc. I've also known people with hypoglycemia (low blood sugar) who had similar physical feelings that have added "second fear" and caused them great difficulty leading to panic. Do get checked out by your physician. It would be in your best interest.

Instead of becoming so alarmed and adding fuel to the fire, I found this formula to be interesting:

A = thought, B = feel, C = behavior.

If A = B and B = C, then A = C.

A = B If we change the way we think, the result can change the way we feel.

B = C If we change the way we feel, the result can change the behavior.

A = C If we change the way we think initially, the result can change the behavior.

The final result is eliminating the panic because changing the thought takes away the panic and the behavior results in no longer running in fear or continuing an avoidance pattern.

Stop adding the "second fear." The "Oh, no, here it is again!" "Will this ever stop?" "What's next?" "Something's terribly wrong with me." "What if…" You have to change the battle of the mind.

2 Corinthians 10:5 "Casting down arguments and every high thing that exalts itself against the knowledge of God, bringing every thought into captivity to the obedience of Christ."

Romans 12:2 "And do not be conformed to this world, but be transformed by the renewing of your mind, that you may prove what is that good and acceptable and perfect will of God."

"Philippians 4:8 "Finally, brethren, whatever things are true, whatever things are noble, whatever things are lovely, whatever things are of good report, if there be any virtue and if there is anything praiseworthy – meditate on these things."

Puzzle Piece Four:
Breathe from the gut.

Over-breathing symptoms consist of dizziness, light-headedness, blurred vision, confusion, and feelings of unreality, numbness, tingling in arms and legs, and cold and clammy hands. I suffered all these sensations and added mental what-ifs to the physical feelings. The blurred vision and feelings of unreality were biggies for me. There's actually a way to calm and relax yourself by retraining your breathing. You can learn to breathe from your diaphragm or abdomen or as I like to refer to it "from the gut."

I was first introduced to this form of breathing by David Rush, psychologist, and later learned more about it. I've modified the instructions below:

- You began by lying down.
- Assume a comfortable position, relax, and take a few seconds to slow down your breathing.
- Expand your abdomen while you inhale, and collapse it as you exhale.
- Continue to breathe slowly, making your exhale more prolonged than your inhale.
- Breathe in through your nose and out through your mouth emphasizing the exhalation by making a long "hah" sound with the mouth open and relaxed.

Of course when in the mall or restaurant you won't be able to lie down and do these exercises, but with practice at home I've found you can do the same breathing techniques unnoticed calming your heart rate along with the other frightening symptoms while you remain in the public setting or wherever you may be. I've worked through my panic by using this breathing method often. One time that comes to mind was during an invitation to dinner with friends who were unaware that I struggled with a phobia. We were seated in the rear of the restaurant, and I began to feel some anxiety creeping in. I used this puzzle piece, calming my whole body down and enjoying the night out. Some times are more difficult than others; but when combining all the puzzle pieces, they blend very well together. It just takes learning each one and implementing them again and again which brings me to my next puzzle piece.

PUZZLE PIECE FIVE:
PRACTICE MAKES PERFECT.

Truly this statement has been around for centuries but the importance of practice is astronomical! Finding the time, or should I say making the time, is so important. I have found in writing this book and reflecting back on the successes I've gained, I can see where the practice came into play. Dr. Claire Weekes advised:

"Practice, practice, practice. Take your journey moment by moment. Regard it as moments to be passed through, not a threatening distance to be covered. See each practice through slowly; no rush. Don't withdraw from panic for an imagined terror, an imagined ultimate! *And never turn back.*"

I couldn't count the times I've turned back...

There is no magic bullet and definitely no magic pill; it is treatable, and your very best weapon is your own hard work and practice. Dr. Weekes wrote numerous times, "Peace is on the other side of panic," and only when you pass through will you find comfort. Use the techniques you've learned.

I was given a book titled, *Triumph Over Fear* written by Jerilyn Ross by a couple that Brad and I grew to love over the years, Larry and Joann Tanner. Since that time, Joann has gone to be with the

Lord. God has blessed Larry with another wonderful wife, Carol, who has supported me and prayed continuous during the writings of this book. However, Larry and Joann learned of my agoraphobia when I struggled to travel to Myrtle Beach to their condo. The book was wonderful; one thing I remember in the writings is that Jerilyn gave the advice of whatever *out* gets you *in*. She explained it in this way: "An out is anything that gets you in. If knowing you can leave in the middle of an event enables you to attend in the first place, it's okay to give yourself that option, or *out*. If thinking you can leave keeps you from feeling trapped and gives you permission in your own mind to enter a situation you may have avoided, even allowing yourself permission to turn the car around and go home if you so choose. Many people will become frustrated if this actually happens while venturing out on vacation, but you're more likely to make the trip if you know you can go home and not forced to stay the route. A word of advice to those helping someone with this fear: *When you force, you only heighten the panic in the person struggling and they are more likely to avoid it in the future.* Later, with the help of this concept, I traveled to Myrtle Beach—making an eight hour trip successfully that I had avoided just a few weeks earlier. Brad expressed to me that at any point if I were so miserable he would turn the car around and go home. I knew that he meant just what he said and that helped me to press on and reach the destiny and enjoy the walk on the beach as the sun set over the ocean. I'm using this concept more and more and instead of turning down invitations I allow myself whatever *out* that gets me *in*.

Puzzle Piece Six:

The greatest of all: God Almighty.

I've spoke of puzzle pieces throughout and how I'm learning to fit each shape into its place on my board, figuratively speaking. Still trying to master each chip of information, I'm learning to unlearn this phobia. Recalling I was instructed in the beginning that I had learned a behavior and now I needed to unlearn my habit of retracting from the fear and wanting to escape the feelings. It's an ongoing process that I continue to instill in my life.

Recovery and success do *not* mean I will never experience anxiety and panic but to no longer let it run my life! Realizing there's hope and letting go of the core beliefs that became embedded as roots intertwined in my soul, living and moving through the fear allowing myself to be put in fearful situations not in the aspect of "getting used to" but knowing how to cope with the panic.

During the years of my panic and agoraphobia, I found it difficult to combine the behavioral skills I was learning from counselors with the teachings of the Bible. I was taught that Jesus Christ overcame the world and that He experienced everything we would ever go through. John 16:33 says, "These things I have spoken to you, that in Me you may have peace. In the world *you will have tribulation*; but be of good cheer, I have overcome the world." I had never read to my knowledge of someone in the scriptures having a panic attack, or let's just say it was never worded that way. I believe the Bible with all my heart, but I couldn't seem to tie my struggles with the readings in God's Word until He shone the light so brilliantly for me when I read Luke 22:39–44:

Coming out, He went to the Mount of Olives, as He was accustomed, and His disciples also followed Him. When He came to the place, He said to them, "Pray that you may not enter into temptation." And He was withdrawn from them about a stone's throw, and He knelt down and prayed, saying, "Father, if it is Your will, take this cup away from Me; nevertheless not My will, but Yours, be done." Then an angel appeared to Him from heaven, strengthening Him. And being in *agony*, He prayed more earnestly, then His sweat became like great drops of blood falling down to the ground.

Agony—Webster's definition: extreme physical or mental pain; the death struggle; throes; pang.

If I ever got a glimpse of Christ having anxiety, it was in these verses. Talk about anticipatory anxiety! I merely thought I was dying and panicked. He was truly facing death on the cross for my sins and the sins of the world. The last moments as He hung on the cross, He spoke the words, "Father, why hast thou forsaken me?" Was He experiencing a panic attack?

I've questioned throughout the adventure of the writing of this book; how would I eventually finalize? And as I reach this point of closure, there is no way I could conclude without pointing my readers to the source of all struggles. The One who comforted me and loved me when I didn't love myself. The One who overcame panic!

The greatest puzzle piece of all: God Almighty. I know God doesn't want me defeated with a life of anxiety, panic, and agoraphobia. He promises never to leave me or forsake me; He never has! Truly He was listening when I prayed, and all the while working in my life, supplying me with "puzzle pieces." And as my mom, who has been the prayer warrior I could only wish to mimic, has taught through her years: "The times you think God didn't answer your prayer, He just said *no* or *wait.*"

In Corinthians 12:7–9, Paul prayed three times that God remove the thorn in his flesh, instead God said, "My grace is sufficient for you, for my strength is made perfect in weakness." He didn't merely just wipe away my struggles with panic and agoraphobia, but He supplied my need and grew me and is still growing me while I continue "with Him" to put the pieces in place.

During the times I've written through tear-filled eyes, God has brought healing to me as well. I'm reminded of a framed quote that sits on my desk that says, "You cannot light the way for others without brightening your own path." For those searching for an answer, for hope, just for someone else to understand your battle and to say, "I've been there; I've walked through this valley; you are not alone."

I am reminded of these words from my sister, Dondra: "You're writing this for the next generation." Unfortunately, panic and agoraphobia continues to rob and infest lives. Since the release of the first book: "Looking for an Exit" God has placed several people in my life that I was able to minister to who also suffered with panic and anxiety. All ages, all walks of life.

If I'm able to shine the light for "such a time as this," **To God be the glory!**

Christmas 2016

BIBLE VERSES AND ONE LAST NOTE

*L*isted below are a few Bible verses that have helped me through the years:

2 Corinthians 10:5, "Casting down arguments and every high thing that exalts itself against the knowledge of God, bringing *every thought into captivity* to the obedience of Christ."

Romans 12:2, "And do not be conformed to this world, but be transformed by the *renewing of your mind*, that you may prove what is that good and acceptable and perfect will of God."

Ephesians 4:23, *"And be renewed in the spirit of your mind."*

Philippians 4:8, "Finally, brethren, whatever things are true, whatever things are noble, whatever things are just, whatever things are pure, whatever things are lovely, whatever things are of *good report*, if there be any virtue and if there is anything praiseworthy—*meditate on these things."*

Isaiah 26:3, "Thou will keep him in *perfect peace*, whose mind is stayed on thee; because he trusts in thee."

Matthew 6:34, "Therefore, *do not worry* about tomorrow, for tomorrow will worry about its own things."

One of my all time favorites: Philippians 4:6, *"Be anxious for nothing, but in everything by prayer and supplication, with thanksgiving, let your requests be made known to God."*

One last note: Words of encouragement from two women I'll always cherish:

Debra Davis Brown, Director Henry County Counseling Center: **"You will never lose the ground you've gained."**

Dr. Claire Weekes (1903–1990): **"My best wishes to you all,** *be off this minute."*

YOUR HEART IS POUNDING. YOU FEEL AS IF YOU CAN'T BREATHE. A STRANGE UNEASINESS TAKES OVER, AND YOUR BODY RAGES WITH FEAR. YOUR MIND IS ENGULFED WITH THE FRIGHTENING THOUGHT: I MUST BE DYING!

*I*f those words strike a chord with you, you might be suffering from panic attacks. If you've began avoiding any place or situations because you feel these sensations, you may have agoraphobia. It's important to know you are not alone. You did not invent this.

Author Lisa Tucker invites you to take a glimpse inside the walls that held her captive for years: a life of panic attacks that led to agoraphobia. Terror paralyzed her.

Many told her to "get a grip." Many, including Lisa, did not understand what was going on with the debilitating panic. It ended her career, and kept her on the outskirts of everything— until she found power over the panic.

While struggling with this gripping fear, she desperately searched for answers that would bring her freedom from her-self-made cell. Honey, you'll think you're dying: it's not death, it's panic sheds light on her experiences and reveals that peace is truly on the other side of panic.

Lisa Tucker lives in Georgia.

Printed in the United States
By Bookmasters